Mastering Financial Investigation:

From Basics to Forensic Expertise

The Guide on How to Become a Financial Investigator

Ann Adams

Unlock the Secrets of Financial Investigations with Our Comprehensive Guide!

Dive into the dynamic world of financial investigations with "Mastering Financial Investigations: From Basics to Forensic Expertise." Whether you're a budding investigator, a seasoned professional, or an academic, this book offers a step-by-step exploration of the complex landscape of financial crimes—from fraud detection to advanced forensic analysis.

Why Choose This Book?

- **Comprehensive Coverage**: From foundational concepts to advanced techniques, this book covers everything you need to know about financial investigations. Understand the critical role of financial stability, learn to navigate the legal intricacies, and master the tools needed to uncover and analyze financial crimes.

- **Expert Knowledge**: Benefit from insights derived from global standards such as the Financial Action Task Force (FATF) and case studies that span across different sectors including government, private, and non-profit organizations.

- **Practical Applications**: Equipped with real-world examples, case studies, and practical exercises, this guide ensures you can apply your learning directly to day-to-day operations or complex cases.

- **Latest Technological Advancements**: Stay ahead in your field with detailed discussions on the use of artificial intelligence, blockchain analysis, and digital forensics in financial investigations.

- **Career Advancement**: With detailed guidance on educational pathways, certification programs, and career progression, this book is an invaluable resource for anyone looking to advance their career in financial investigation.

Who Will Benefit?

- Law Enforcement Officers keen on specializing in financial crimes.
- Financial Professionals in banking, insurance, and other sectors who need to understand the forensic side of finance.
- Students and Academics looking for a comprehensive textbook on financial crime investigation.
- Legal Professionals needing a deeper understanding of financial legislations and fraudulent practices.

"Mastering Financial Investigations" is more than just a textbook—it's a toolkit for building a successful career in safeguarding economic integrity. Equip yourself with the knowledge and skills to become a proficient financial investigator and make a substantial impact in the world of finance.

Get your copy today and start mastering the art of financial investigation!

Table of Contents

Introduction 9
   Overview of Financial Investigation 9
   Why This Book? 11
   What You Will Achieve 13

Chapter 1: The Role of a Financial Investigator 17
   1.1 Understanding Your Role 19
   1.2 Scope of Work 24
   1.3 Setting the Right Expectations 27

Chapter 2: Fundamentals of Financial Crimes 32
   2.1 Defining Financial Crimes 34
   2.2 Tools of the Trade 42
   2.3 Legal Frameworks 46

Chapter 3: Preparing for Financial Investigations 52
   3.1 Educational and Background Requirements 55
   3.2 Legal and Ethical Considerations 58
   3.3 Setting Up Your Workspace 62

Chapter 4: Investigative Techniques and Approaches .. 67
   4.1 Standard Investigative Techniques 72
   4.2 Advanced Investigative Techniques 77
   4.3 Special Investigative Measures 82

Chapter 5: Advanced Investigative Strategies 87
   5.1 Developing a Strategic Investigation Plan 90
   5.2 Leveraging Technological Advancements 94
   5.3 Case Management Techniques 99

Chapter 6: Working with Financial Institutions 104
   6.1 Understanding Financial Systems 106
   6.2 Gathering Intelligence from Financial Institutions 111

6.3 Building Relationships with Bank Compliance Officers and Other Insiders 115

Chapter 7: International and Multi-jurisdictional Investigations 120

7.1 Challenges of Global Financial Crime 122

7.2 Building International Cooperation 126

7.3 Using Technology to Bridge Gaps 130

Chapter 8: Communication and Reporting 135

8.1 Effective Communication Skills 138

8.2 Writing Detailed Reports 143

8.3 Handling the Media 148

Chapter 9: Building a Network of Trust 153

9.1 Establishing Trustworthy Connections 157

9.2 Inter-agency Collaboration 160

9.3 International Networks 164

Chapter 10: Future Trends and Career Advancement 168

10.1 Navigating Emerging Trends in Financial Crime 171

10.2 Career Advancement in Financial Investigation .. 175

10.3 Innovations in Financial Investigation 180

Conclusion 186

Final Thoughts 193

List of References: 197

Introduction

Overview of Financial Investigation

Financial investigation is a specialized field of inquiry that plays a crucial role in uncovering financial crimes and ensuring the integrity of financial systems around the world. Unlike traditional criminal investigations, which may focus on direct offenses such as theft or assault, financial investigations delve into the complexities of economic transactions to detect and thwart white-collar crimes like fraud, embezzlement, and money laundering. This form of investigation has become increasingly significant as economies grow more intertwined and as financial systems evolve with advancing technology.

The importance of financial investigations extends beyond the prosecution of crimes. These investigations also protect public and private resources, maintain systemic trust among market participants, and uphold the rule of law. Financial investigators are thus the custodians of financial stability, diligently working behind the scenes to ensure that economies function efficiently and are not undermined by illicit activities.

Financial investigations differ from traditional criminal investigations in several ways. Firstly, the nature of the crime is often hidden deep within layers of legitimate business transactions, requiring a different set of investigative skills focused on forensic accounting, data analysis, and intricate legal knowledge. Secondly, the scope of financial investigations is usually broader, with potential international implications due to the cross-border nature of many financial transactions today. Lastly, the evidence in financial crimes is primarily documentary, often buried in mountains of data and requiring sophisticated tools to decode.

This book is structured to guide you through the essential knowledge and skills needed to become an effective financial investigator. Starting from the basics of understanding what financial crimes are, to advanced investigative strategies, the book will provide a step-by-step approach to mastering this complex field. Each chapter is designed to build on the previous one, gradually increasing in complexity and detail. By the end of this book, readers can expect to have a thorough understanding of the role of a financial investigator, the tools and techniques used in the field, legal and ethical considerations, and the latest trends and technologies shaping the future of financial investigations.

Whether you are a law enforcement officer aiming to specialize in financial crimes, a professional in the financial sector looking to enhance your analytic capabilities, or a student considering a career in this dynamic field, this book will serve as a comprehensive guide and reference to help you achieve your goals. By engaging actively with the material presented, you will develop not only the technical skills required for financial investigations but also an analytical mindset that is critical for success in this profession. Through practical examples, case studies, and expert insights, this book aims to equip you with the knowledge and skills necessary to commence or advance your career in financial investigation, fostering a proactive approach to combating financial crime.

Why This Book?

In today's complex economic landscape, the demand for skilled financial investigators has never been higher. As financial systems become increasingly digital and interconnected, the opportunities for financial malpractices have also escalated, underscoring the need for competent investigators who can navigate this intricate environment. This book is crafted to meet the growing demand in both personal and professional realms, providing readers with the foundational knowledge and advanced skills necessary to thrive in the field of financial investigation.

Real-World Applications and Career Opportunities

Financial investigation is not just a niche area within law enforcement; it has broad applications across various sectors. In the private sector, corporations employ financial investigators to safeguard against fraud and to comply with regulatory requirements. Government agencies rely on these professionals to combat everything from tax evasion to international money laundering. Non-profits and educational institutions also benefit from the expertise of financial investigators to ensure the proper stewardship of funds. The career opportunities in this field are thus vast and varied, offering paths that can suit different interests and skills, ranging from forensic accounting to cybersecurity finance roles.

Moreover, the skills you learn as a financial investigator—such as analytical thinking, attention to detail, and a deep understanding of financial mechanisms—are highly transferrable and sought after in many other areas. This book not only prepares you to enter the field of financial investigation but also equips you with expertise that can elevate your professional profile in a variety of career paths.

Encouragement to Engage Actively

This book is designed to be interactive, encouraging readers to engage actively with the material. Through practical exercises, real-world case studies, and critical thinking assignments, you will be able to apply what you learn directly to various scenarios. This active engagement is crucial for deepening your understanding and enhancing your investigative skills. Each chapter includes components that challenge you to think like a financial investigator, making theoretical knowledge tangible through practical application.

Furthermore, this book serves as a comprehensive guide that addresses the current and future needs of the financial investigation profession. By staying abreast of technological advancements and understanding evolving financial crime methodologies, you will be better prepared to adapt and thrive in this dynamic field.

Connecting back to the overview provided earlier, this book lays down a systematic approach to becoming a proficient financial investigator. Starting with the basics and progressing to complex investigative techniques, the journey through these pages is both educational and transformative, aiming to mold novices into experts capable of making a significant impact in the world of finance and beyond.

What You Will Achieve

Embarking on the journey through this book will equip you with a robust set of tools and knowledge, positioning you to conduct effective financial investigations and advance within this challenging field. By integrating insights and research from esteemed organizations such as the World Bank, United Nations, Financial Action Task Force (FATF), Egmont Group, Basel Committee, and Wolfsberg Group, this text ensures that your learning is grounded in the most current and globally recognized standards.

Practical Skills for Conducting Effective Financial Investigations

This book provides hands-on training in the essential practices of financial investigation. You will learn how to scrutinize financial records, perform forensic data analysis, and employ advanced investigative techniques. For instance, the World Bank and UNODC's StAR Initiative (Stolen Asset Recovery) highlights the necessity for skills in tracking and recovering illicit financial flows as a measure against corruption and crime. Through exercises and examples inspired by real-world scenarios, you will acquire the ability to navigate complex financial systems and uncover hidden financial relationships.

Understanding Legal Frameworks and Procedural Requirements

A fundamental part of your training will involve understanding the legal frameworks that govern financial investigations. This includes national laws and international protocols that shape how investigations are conducted across borders. The FATF, for instance, provides a series of recommendations that are recognized as the international standard for combating money laundering and terrorist financing. This book distills these complex legal standards into practical knowledge, ensuring that you are well-versed in compliance and procedural requirements. Furthermore, guidelines from the Basel Committee on Banking Supervision and the Wolfsberg Group's principles on anti-money laundering (AML) and counter-terrorism financing (CTF) will be discussed to provide a thorough grounding in regulatory expectations and ethical standards.

Preparation for Advanced Roles in Financial Investigation and Analysis

As you progress through the book, you will be prepared not just to participate in but to lead financial investigations. This includes training on the use of sophisticated investigative technologies and methodologies, such as those endorsed by the Egmont Group—a united body of 166 Financial Intelligence Units that emphasizes the importance of secure and efficient exchange of financial intelligence. By understanding these advanced tools and practices, you will be poised to take on senior roles within government, private sector, and international organizations, tackling some of the most pressing financial crimes of our time.

Through these chapters, you will not only learn from detailed theoretical frameworks but also from extensive case studies and industry reports that reflect the latest research and developments in the field. This comprehensive approach ensures that by the end of this book, you will have not only mastered the practical aspects of financial investigation but also appreciated the broader implications of your work on global economic security and justice.

Chapter 1: The Role of a Financial Investigator

In the intricate and ever-evolving world of finance, the role of a financial investigator stands out as a crucial element in the fight against economic crime. This chapter delves into the critical responsibilities and varied environments in which financial investigators operate, highlighting the indispensable role they play in safeguarding the integrity of financial systems globally. By exploring the depth and breadth of this career, you will gain a comprehensive understanding of what it means to be a financial investigator, the significant impact you can have, and the skills necessary to succeed.

Financial investigators are the frontline defenders against complex financial crimes. They are tasked with uncovering activities that could undermine the financial stability of businesses, governments, and non-profits alike. The role is critical not only in terms of identifying and responding to incidents of fraud, embezzlement, and money laundering but also in preventing these crimes before they occur. Through detailed analysis and a thorough understanding of financial systems, investigators play a pivotal role in enforcing laws and regulations designed to protect market integrity and promote transparency.

The work of a financial investigator varies widely depending on the sector and specific job responsibilities. Whether working within government agencies, private corporations, or non-profit organizations, financial investigators encounter a range of cases from intricate money laundering schemes to straightforward instances of corporate fraud. This section will provide a glimpse into the day-to-day activities as well as the long-term projects that define a career in financial investigation, supplemented by a case study that illustrates a typical day in the life of a financial investigator.

While the career of a financial investigator can be incredibly rewarding, it comes with its own set of challenges. This section addresses common misconceptions about the workload and the emotional and mental impact of the job. It also discusses the potential for career growth within the field, offering insights into how financial investigators can advance their careers through skill enhancement and specialization. Understanding these dynamics will prepare you for a successful and fulfilling career in financial investigation, equipped with realistic expectations and a clear vision of the road ahead.

By the end of this chapter, you will have a solid foundation of the role and responsibilities of a financial investigator, enriched with practical insights and real-world applications, setting the stage for deeper exploration into the techniques, challenges, and rewards of this vital profession.

1.1 Understanding Your Role

The role of a financial investigator is pivotal in combating financial crimes, a field that has grown in complexity and scope with the expansion of global financial markets. Financial investigators serve as guardians of economic stability, tasked with detecting, preventing, and responding to a range of illicit activities that can undermine the integrity of financial systems and erode public trust.

Financial investigations are an essential mechanism for detecting money laundering, terrorist financing, and other significant criminal activities. These investigations serve as a critical resource for generating new leads that help unveil hidden criminal activities and delineate entire criminal networks, including their international connections. Moreover, they provide crucial evidence for prosecuting suspects, and for identifying and seizing criminal assets.

Financial investigations involve a detailed examination of the financial aspects related to criminal conduct. Their goal is to identify, analyze, and interpret relevant financial data for use in criminal proceedings. With the rising threat of legitimate economies being infiltrated by serious and organized crime, financial investigations are vital for a modern and effective strategy to combat criminal and terrorist threats.This section explores the critical nature of the position, the various sectors where these professionals are needed, and the essential qualities and skills required to excel in this challenging and rewarding career.

The Critical Nature of the Position

Financial crimes such as fraud, money laundering, and corruption have significant implications for economic and social stability. They can drain national wealth, destabilize markets, and divert resources from beneficial uses. The role of financial investigators is therefore crucial in safeguarding the financial system against these threats. By meticulously tracing financial transactions, identifying irregularities, and gathering evidence, these investigators help to enforce laws and regulations that are designed to maintain market integrity and protect public and private assets.

For example, in the fight against money laundering, financial investigators work to disrupt the mechanisms that allow illegal earnings to enter the mainstream financial system, thereby curbing the underlying criminal activities that generate these funds, such as drug trafficking or terrorism financing. Their work not only helps in apprehending criminals but also in deterring future financial crimes through the demonstration of effective oversight and accountability.

Various Sectors Needing Financial Investigators

Financial investigators are integral across multiple sectors:

- **Government**: In government agencies, financial investigators may work for tax authorities, customs agencies, or financial intelligence units. Their investigations support the prosecution of tax evasion, fraud against the government, bribery of public officials, and more complex crimes like organized crime and terrorist financing.

- **Private Sector**: Within the private sector, corporations employ financial investigators to prevent and detect internal fraud and ensure compliance with financial regulations. These roles are particularly critical in banking, insurance, and other financial services industries where large sums of money are managed and regulatory oversight is stringent.

- **Non-profits**: Non-profit organizations also require the expertise of financial investigators to prevent misuse of funds and ensure that donations are used as intended. This is vital not only for legal compliance but also for maintaining donor trust and organizational credibility.

Essential Qualities and Skills of a Successful Financial Investigator

To be effective in their role, financial investigators must possess a specific set of qualities and skills:

- **Analytical Skills**: The ability to analyze complex data sets and identify anomalies that may indicate criminal activity is fundamental. Financial investigators must discern patterns within vast amounts of financial data to spot inconsistencies that warrant further investigation.

- **Attention to Detail**: Given that financial crimes can involve intricate networks and subtle transactional signs, meticulous attention to detail is crucial in following through on potential leads and in documenting investigative processes for legal proceedings.

- **Integrity and Ethics**: Strong ethical standards are essential, as financial investigators often handle sensitive information and must do so with honesty and professionalism to maintain the credibility of their investigations.

- **Communication Skills**: Effective communication is necessary for articulating findings clearly and persuasively, whether in written reports or oral presentations. Financial investigators must also be adept at interviewing and gathering information from various sources.

- **Technical Proficiency**: In an era where financial transactions are increasingly digital, proficiency with specialized software and investigative tools is necessary for conducting effective investigations.

- **Legal Knowledge**: Understanding the legal frameworks within which financial crimes operate is critical. Knowledge of laws related to financial oversight, such as anti-money laundering (AML) statutes, is particularly important.

By embodying these qualities and continually developing these skills, financial investigators can significantly impact the detection and prevention of financial crimes, contributing to broader economic and social well-being. As this field evolves, so too must the strategies and approaches of those entrusted with this critical responsibility, ensuring they remain effective guardians of the financial system.

1.2 Scope of Work

The scope of work for a financial investigator encompasses a broad range of responsibilities and tasks, each critical to the effective detection and prevention of financial crimes. This subchapter provides an in-depth look at the types of cases typically handled by financial investigators, explores their day-to-day responsibilities, and illustrates these concepts through a detailed case study. This exploration not only highlights the diversity and complexity of the work involved but also sheds light on the essential tools and methodologies employed in the field.

Types of Cases Typically Handled

Financial investigators tackle a wide array of cases, each with its unique challenges and requirements:

- **Money Laundering**: Investigators track the movement of illicit funds through the financial system, working to intercept these flows and identify the individuals and networks behind them. This often involves unraveling complex layers of transactions spread across multiple countries and legal jurisdictions.

- **Corporate Fraud**: In cases of corporate fraud, investigators look into misrepresentations, false financial statements, and other deceitful corporate practices that can lead to significant financial losses and damage to investor confidence. These investigations might involve insider trading, accounting fraud, and embezzlement.

- **Tax Evasion**: Tax-related investigations focus on uncovering deliberate attempts by individuals or corporations to evade tax liabilities. This includes investigating offshore accounts, shell companies, and other strategies used to hide taxable assets.

- **Bribery and Corruption**: Financial investigators are also crucial in exposing bribery and corruption, especially within public sectors where they help ensure that government officials and departments operate transparently and lawfully.

Day-to-Day Responsibilities

The daily responsibilities of a financial investigator vary significantly based on their specific role and the sector in which they operate. Common daily tasks include:

- **Data Analysis**: A significant portion of a financial investigator's day involves analyzing financial data and records to identify irregularities that may suggest criminal activity. This process is supported by advanced software tools that can process and visualize large datasets.

- **Interviews and Information Gathering**: Conducting interviews with suspects, witnesses, and informants is crucial for gathering insights and corroborating data gathered during investigations.

- **Report Writing**: Documenting findings in detailed reports is essential, not only for legal processes but also for record-keeping and reference in future investigations.

- **Collaboration and Coordination**: Financial investigators often work in teams and must coordinate with other departments and agencies, including law enforcement, regulatory bodies, and international organizations, to effectively manage cases.

Case Study: A Day in the Life of a Financial Investigator

To illustrate the scope of work, consider a case study of a financial investigator named Alex, who specializes in anti-money laundering efforts within a major banking institution. Alex starts their day reviewing transactions flagged overnight by the bank's automated systems as suspicious. Each transaction is scrutinized for patterns that might indicate money laundering, such as small, frequent transfers or transfers to high-risk jurisdictions.

After identifying a potentially dubious series of transactions, Alex consults with colleagues from the compliance and legal departments to discuss the findings. The team decides to escalate the case, and Alex prepares a detailed report summarizing the evidence, which will be submitted to the national financial intelligence unit.

In the afternoon, Alex conducts a training session for new bank employees, emphasizing the importance of vigilance in monitoring customer transactions. The day concludes with Alex updating the case management system, scheduling follow-up tasks, and preparing for a presentation to senior management about emerging money laundering trends and how the bank can better safeguard against them.

This case study demonstrates the multifaceted nature of a financial investigator's role, combining analytical tasks, collaborative efforts, and educational responsibilities, all of which are crucial for maintaining the integrity of financial systems and combating financial crime effectively. Through such detailed insights, this subchapter aims to prepare readers for the diverse and dynamic challenges they will face as financial investigators.

1.3 Setting the Right Expectations

Embarking on a career as a financial investigator involves not only understanding the scope of your responsibilities but also setting realistic expectations about the challenges and rewards that come with the role. This subchapter explores common misconceptions about the workload and impact of financial investigators, outlines the typical career trajectory in this field, and highlights the personal and professional growth that can be expected from this demanding yet rewarding career.

Challenges and Rewards of a Career in Financial Investigation

Challenges:
- **Complexity of Cases**: Financial investigators often deal with highly complex cases that require a deep understanding of financial systems and criminal behavior. These cases can be prolonged and intricate, demanding high levels of concentration and expertise.

- **Emotional and Mental Stress**: The nature of the work, which often involves dealing with criminal activities and sometimes corruption within trusted institutions, can be emotionally taxing. Financial investigators need to maintain a high level of professional integrity and emotional detachment to effectively handle their duties.

- **High Expectations for Accuracy and Detail**: The outcomes of financial investigations can have significant legal and financial implications. As such, there is little room for error, and investigators are expected to perform their duties with utmost accuracy and attention to detail.

Rewards:

- **Impact on Financial Integrity**: Financial investigators play a key role in maintaining or restoring the integrity of financial systems. Their work helps prevent and address financial crimes, contributing significantly to the stability and transparency of financial markets.

- **Career Advancement Opportunities**: This field offers diverse opportunities for advancement, from specializing in certain types of financial crimes to moving into higher management roles. Experienced investigators are highly valued for their specialized knowledge and are often sought after for senior positions within both public and private sectors.

- **Continuous Learning and Skill Development**: The field of financial investigation is dynamic, with new technologies and methods constantly emerging. Professionals in this field have the opportunity to continuously develop their skills and knowledge, keeping pace with the latest advancements in digital forensics, cybersecurity, and financial regulations.

Common Misconceptions

- Misconception: The Work Is Primarily Reactive: While it is true that financial investigators must respond to alerts and incidents of financial crimes, a significant part of their work is also proactive. This includes developing better systems and processes to detect potential financial crimes before they occur.
- Misconception: It's All About Numbers: While financial acumen is crucial, the role also requires strong investigative skills, the ability to understand human behavior, and effective communication skills. The best financial investigators are not just good with numbers but also with people.

Career Trajectory and Potential Growth

The typical career path for a financial investigator can vary widely based on the sector and individual interests. Starting positions might involve basic data analysis and monitoring transactions. As investigators gain experience, they may take on more complex investigations, lead investigative teams, or specialize in a particular type of financial crime, such as anti-money laundering, tax evasion, or corporate fraud.

For those interested in leadership, opportunities exist to move into managerial roles, overseeing entire departments dedicated to fraud prevention, compliance, or risk management. Additionally, some investigators choose to leverage their skills in consultancy roles, advising firms on best practices for fraud prevention and financial integrity.

This subchapter aims to provide a realistic picture of what aspiring financial investigators can expect from their career—both the good and the challenging—enabling them to approach the field with a balanced perspective and clear expectations. By understanding these dynamics, individuals can better prepare themselves for a successful and impactful career in financial investigation.

Chapter 2: Fundamentals of Financial Crimes

Financial crime represents a multi-trillion-dollar enterprise for criminal organizations globally. The United Nations Office on Drugs and Crime estimates that annually up to $2 trillion in illicit funds are laundered through international financial networks, accounting for two to five percent of the global GDP—a figure that continues to rise each year. Alarmingly, it is estimated that only one percent of these illicit financial flows are successfully intercepted on a global scale.

Criminals are increasingly inventive in devising methods to commit financial crimes, influenced significantly by local economic conditions, financial markets, and the specific anti-money laundering (AML) and counter-financing of terrorism (CFT) regulations in their operational regions. Moreover, the intricate nature of financial services often complicates the detection and prevention of such activities.

Additionally, large-scale organized crime syndicates, which operate internationally, exploit variances in national criminal laws to their advantage.

Understanding the fundamentals of financial crimes is the cornerstone of a career in financial investigation. This chapter provides a thorough exploration of what constitutes financial crime, the impact these crimes have on economies and societies, and the historical evolution of illicit financial activities. By dissecting the nature and mechanics of various financial crimes, this chapter equips readers with the foundational knowledge needed to recognize and combat these offenses effectively.

Financial crimes encompass a broad range of illegal acts, from money laundering and fraud to bribery and tax evasion. These activities not only weaken the financial systems but also undermine the economic stability and security of nations. The tactics used by criminals are becoming increasingly sophisticated, leveraging new technologies and global financial networks to evade detection. Therefore, it is imperative for financial investigators to understand both the traditional and emerging methodologies used in financial crimes to stay one step ahead.

This chapter will delve into several key areas:

- **Defining Financial Crimes**: A clear definition and classification of financial crimes will be provided to set the foundation for deeper understanding. This section will outline the various types of financial crimes and the legal frameworks used to categorize and combat them.

- **Impact on Economies and Societies**: Discussion of how financial crimes affect economies at both macro and micro levels, including their effects on businesses, governments, and individuals. This section will also cover the social implications of financial crimes, such as loss of public trust and damage to institutional integrity.

- **Historical Perspectives**: By examining landmark cases and significant shifts in the legal treatment of financial crimes over the years, this section will offer insights into how regulatory responses have evolved and what lessons can be learned from past incidents.

Through detailed exploration and case studies, this chapter aims to provide a comprehensive overview of the fundamentals of financial crimes, setting the stage for deeper dives into investigative techniques and legal frameworks in subsequent chapters. By the end of this chapter, readers will possess a solid understanding of the complexities surrounding financial crimes and be better prepared to engage in effective prevention and investigative efforts.

2.1 Defining Financial Crimes

Financial crimes are a diverse category of illegal acts, primarily involving the manipulation or misuse of financial systems to gain illicit benefits. These crimes can range from fraud and embezzlement to money laundering and tax evasion. This subchapter aims to define and categorize these acts clearly, setting a solid foundation for understanding the mechanisms and motivations behind these crimes, as well as the legal frameworks designed to combat them.

What Constitutes a Financial Crime?

Financial crimes typically involve an offender using deceit or theft to obtain or conceal financial resources. The complexity of these crimes can vary significantly—from straightforward theft or fraud by an individual to sophisticated schemes operated across international borders by organized crime syndicates. Here are some of the most common types of financial crimes:

- **Fraud**: This involves the use of deception to gain unjust advantage financially. Examples include credit card fraud, insurance fraud, and securities fraud.

- **Money Laundering**: Money laundering is a financial crime designed to disguise the origins of money obtained through illicit activities. The primary goal is to introduce the criminally-derived money into the financial system, a process known as placement. The next step involves layering or structuring, where the money is shuffled through numerous transactions to create a complex trail that appears legitimate and makes it challenging to trace back to its criminal source. The final phase, integration, involves reintroducing the laundered money back into the economy, allowing criminals to use the funds without drawing scrutiny from authorities.

- **Terrorist Financing**: Terrorist financing involves the provision of financial assets to terrorists, including both individuals and groups, to support their activities such as purchasing weapons and supplies necessary for executing attacks on civilians.

Given the severe penalties associated with aiding terrorists, those who finance terrorism often employ tactics similar to those used in money laundering. They attempt to covertly introduce assets into legitimate financial systems and obscure the origins and destinations of these funds to avoid detection and prosecution.

- **Embezzlement**: This occurs when an individual or entity, entrusted with or granted access to funds designated for specific purposes, illicitly diverts those funds for personal use or unauthorized ends. This may involve transferring the funds to personal accounts or to those of third parties, often accompanied by the creation of fraudulent invoices or receipts to conceal the illicit activity. Embezzlement can take place within organizations and can vary widely in scale, from minor thefts to extensive schemes involving millions of dollars.

- **Tax Evasion**: Tax evasion is a financial crime that involves intentionally not paying or underpaying taxes. Methods of committing tax evasion include deliberately failing to report taxable income, falsely claiming more deductions than are legally permissible, or choosing not to file a tax return at all.

Entities may also engage in tax evasion by placing or investing their assets in foreign banks or shell companies—entities that may lack a physical presence or active operations. This strategy is often used to misrepresent the true amount of assets owned, thereby illegally reducing the tax liability owed.

- **Bribery and Corruption**: Corruption involves individuals in positions of power who abuse their roles to unlawfully obtain advantages, including financial benefits, for themselves or others. This abuse of power can encompass acts of embezzlement and may also involve bribery.

Bribery represents one aspect of corruption where individuals or entities illegally offer financial benefits to authorities in exchange for favorable treatment in decisions that impact the public. For instance, a company might pay off officials in a country to secure permission to operate there while circumventing the required regulatory standards.

- **Cybercrime**: As financial transactions increasingly migrate online, so too does financial crime. Cybercriminals are exploiting digital channels to engage in a wide range of illicit activities, including theft of money and authentication credentials, exposure of confidential information, forgery and counterfeiting of financial assets, market manipulation, and various forms of fraud.

Virtual currencies, in particular, have become prominent tools in financial crime. This popularity is driven by several factors, including the relative lack of regulatory oversight, the semi-anonymous nature of transactions, and the decentralized administration of these currencies via blockchain technology, which makes transactions irreversible once executed.

Consequently, virtual currencies are frequently involved in financial crimes such as market manipulation, money laundering, terrorist financing, tax evasion, and other fraudulent schemes.

- **Insider Trading and Market Abuse**: Sometimes, individuals or entities engage in the illegal practice of insider trading by using confidential information about a company's financial status to buy or sell securities. This constitutes a financial crime in many jurisdictions because the trader typically has access to this sensitive information through a position of trust, or they have illicitly obtained it, thereby gaining an unfair advantage over the public who is unaware of these details.

Additionally, there are other illicit methods to manipulate the stock market. For instance, "wash trading" involves buying and immediately reselling shares of a company to create false impressions of high trading volume, which can artificially inflate the stock's price.

Another common manipulation tactic is known as "pump and dump." In this scheme, an entity will buy shares of a low-valued stock and then disseminate rumors or misleading information to suggest the stock's value will soon rise. This misinformation aims to spur a surge in trading activity, temporarily boosting the stock's price. The perpetrators then sell their shares at the inflated price before the market corrects itself when the deception is uncovered, and the stock value returns to normal levels.

Legal Frameworks for Combating Financial Crimes

Financial crimes are governed by a myriad of laws and regulations, both at national and international levels. Understanding these legal frameworks is crucial for financial investigators as they navigate through their investigative processes. Key elements include:

- **Anti-Money Laundering Laws (AML)**: These laws require financial institutions to monitor clients' transactions and report activities that they suspect might be money laundering. The Financial Action Task Force (FATF) provides international standards for combating money laundering and terrorist financing.

- **Anti-Bribery and Corruption Laws**: These include laws like the U.S. Foreign Corrupt Practices Act (FCPA) and the UK Bribery Act, which focus on reducing corruption in business practices, especially in international activities.

- **Securities Laws**: Enforced by regulatory bodies such as the U.S. Securities and Exchange Commission (SEC) and the Financial Conduct Authority (FCA) in the UK, these laws regulate the stock markets and protect investors from fraud.

- **Tax Codes**: National tax codes provide the legal basis for tax-related investigations, stipulating the obligations of taxpayers and the penalties for evasion.

Impact of Financial Crimes

The impact of financial crimes extends far beyond the immediate financial losses incurred by individuals and businesses. They have significant effects on the economies and societies at large:

- **Economic Impact**: Financial crimes can lead to substantial financial losses for businesses, distort financial markets, and increase the costs of operations as companies invest more in security measures and insurance premiums.

- **Social Impact**: These crimes often undermine public trust in financial and governmental institutions. Corruption and bribery, for example, can erode social cohesion and lead to a loss of public confidence in the fairness and effectiveness of public administration and services.

- **Global Consequences**: Especially with crimes like money laundering and tax evasion, there are broader international implications, including the undermining of international financial systems and the financing of terrorism.

Case Studies and Historical Perspectives

To illustrate the breadth and depth of financial crimes, let's consider a few historical case studies:

- **The Enron Scandal (2001)**: This case involved massive accounting fraud at high levels of the corporation, leading to billions of dollars reported in false earnings. It led to significant reforms in financial reporting laws in the United States, including the Sarbanes-Oxley Act.

- **The Panama Papers (2016)**: This was a leak of over 11.5 million financial documents that detailed financial and attorney-client information for more than 214,488 offshore entities. The documents contained personal financial information about wealthy individuals and public officials that had previously been kept private. Investigations led to the recovery of over a billion dollars worldwide, highlighting the global scale of tax evasion and the importance of international cooperation in tackling these issues.

By understanding the definitions, legal frameworks, and impacts of financial crimes, along with examining historical cases, financial investigators can better prepare to tackle these crimes effectively. This foundational knowledge is not only critical for performing their daily responsibilities but also essential for advancing their careers in areas requiring deeper expertise in financial crime prevention and investigation.

2.2 Tools of the Trade

Financial investigations require a sophisticated set of tools and technologies to efficiently detect and analyze financial crimes. This subchapter delves into the key tools and technologies that are fundamental to modern financial investigations, ranging from basic accounting software to advanced digital forensics. It also discusses the importance of staying current with evolving tools to ensure investigators can adeptly handle the increasingly complex nature of financial crimes.

Core Tools and Technologies

Financial investigators rely on a variety of tools to perform their duties effectively. Here's a breakdown of some of the most crucial ones:

- **Accounting Software**: Tools like QuickBooks, Xero, and other specialized forensic accounting software help investigators examine financial records, track transactions, and identify discrepancies that may indicate fraudulent activity.

- **Data Analysis Tools**: Software such as ACL Analytics, IDEA, or even advanced Excel functions allows investigators to perform complex data analysis. These tools can sift through large datasets to find patterns, anomalies, and correlations that might not be visible otherwise.

- Digital Forensics Tools: Applications like EnCase, FTK, or Cellebrite are used in digital forensic investigations to recover deleted files and access encrypted data. These tools are essential in today's digital age, where much financial activity occurs online, and much evidence is stored electronically.

- Database Management Systems: Financial investigators often use database systems like SQL to manage and query large amounts of data. Proficiency in these systems enables investigators to extract and manipulate data effectively for their investigations.

- Visual Analytics Tools: Software like Tableau or Microsoft Power BI is used for visual data analysis. These tools help investigators create visual representations of financial data, making it easier to communicate complex information clearly and quickly identify trends and outliers.

Keeping Current with Technology

The landscape of financial crimes is continually evolving, particularly with the rise of cryptocurrencies and blockchain technology, which pose new challenges and avenues for financial crimes. Financial investigators must stay updated with the latest developments in both the financial industry and technology to remain effective. This involves:

- **Continuous Learning**: Engaging in ongoing education and training programs to learn about new tools and techniques as they develop. This might include attending workshops, seminars, and industry conferences focused on financial investigation and technology.

- **Networking**: Collaborating with peers and technology experts to exchange knowledge about emerging tools and methods. Networking can provide insights into practical applications and best practices in the use of new technologies.

- **Research**: Keeping abreast of the latest research in financial crimes and investigative technologies through journals, academic publications, and professional associations. This research often provides the first look at emerging trends and the tools developed to address them.

Practical Applications

To illustrate the application of these tools, consider a hypothetical scenario: A financial investigator is tasked with uncovering potential embezzlement within a large corporation. By using forensic accounting software, the investigator analyzes the company's financial records and identifies irregular transactions. They then apply data analysis tools to dig deeper into these transactions, uncovering a pattern of misappropriation linked to a specific department. Digital forensics tools help recover deleted emails that confirm the fraudulent activity, and visual analytics tools are used to prepare a report that clearly illustrates the flow of misappropriated funds for presentation in court.

This practical application shows how different tools can be integrated to address complex investigative challenges. By mastering these tools, financial investigators enhance their capability to uncover and document financial crimes effectively, making them invaluable assets in the fight against financial crime.

In summary, the tools and technologies in financial investigation are critical to the detection, analysis, and prosecution of financial crimes. By maintaining proficiency in these tools and staying updated with technological advancements, financial investigators can significantly enhance their effectiveness and adaptability in this dynamic field.

2.3 Legal Frameworks

A deep understanding of the legal frameworks that govern financial crimes is essential for every financial investigator. This subchapter examines the international and national laws and regulations that outline the legal boundaries within which financial crimes are prosecuted. It discusses the role these legal frameworks play in shaping investigative processes and the importance of understanding jurisdictional differences in the enforcement of these laws.

Overview of Key Legal Standards

Financial crimes are regulated by a complex web of laws and regulations, which can vary significantly from one jurisdiction to another. However, some key legal standards have global relevance and are crucial for any financial investigator to understand:

- **Anti-Money Laundering (AML) Laws**: Globally, the Financial Action Task Force (FATF) sets international standards for combating money laundering and terrorist financing. Countries implement these standards through national laws that require financial institutions to perform due diligence on their clients, monitor transactions, and report suspicious activities.

- **Anti-Bribery and Corruption Laws**: These include the U.S. Foreign Corrupt Practices Act (FCPA) and the UK Bribery Act, which have international reach and prohibit the bribery of foreign officials and require companies to maintain accurate books and records.

- **Securities and Exchange Regulations**: These regulations are designed to protect investors, maintain fair, orderly, and efficient markets, and facilitate capital formation. Examples include the U.S. Securities Exchange Act and the European Market Abuse Regulation.

- **Tax Laws**: National tax laws govern the conditions under which taxes must be paid. International agreements and treaties can also play a role, especially in the context of tax evasion and the use of offshore financial centers.

The 2021 EU Strategy for combating organized crime emphasizes the importance of fostering a culture of early financial investigations across all EU nations and enhancing the capabilities of investigators to address the financial aspects of organized crime. This approach aims to eradicate the profits derived from organized crime and prevent its infiltration into the legal economy and society.

EU countries have acknowledged the significance of the "follow the money" strategy in tackling the financial dimensions of organized crime and in discovering new leads during investigations, as outlined in the 2020 Council conclusions on enhancing financial investigations to combat serious and organized crime. These conclusions, which build upon the 2016 Council Conclusion and Action Plan on financial investigations, urge EU nations to integrate financial investigations into all types of criminal probes related to organized crime.

Moreover, financial investigations play a pivotal role in combating terrorism and its funding. Tracking financial transactions helps investigators uncover previously unknown connections in counter-terrorism cases. In the 2020 Counter-Terrorism Agenda, the Commission proposed the creation of a network of counter-terrorism financial investigators. This network would facilitate the sharing of investigative techniques and experiences, enhancing investigators' ability to analyze and understand trends and emerging risks in financial investigations.

Importance of Understanding Jurisdictional Differences

The enforcement of financial crime laws can vary greatly by country due to differences in legal systems, the strength of institutions, and local priorities. Financial investigators must be aware of these differences, especially when dealing with transnational crimes involving multiple jurisdictions. For example, what constitutes a legal financial practice in one country might be illegal in another, and the penalties for the same financial crime can vary widely.

Understanding these jurisdictional differences is critical not only for conducting thorough and lawful investigations but also for collaborating effectively with international counterparts. This might involve navigating extradition treaties, sharing evidence across borders, and coordinating joint operations with international law enforcement agencies.

Legal Challenges in Financial Investigations

Financial investigators often face significant legal challenges, including:

- **Privacy and Data Protection Laws**: These laws can restrict access to financial data and personal information, complicating the task of gathering evidence. Investigators must navigate these laws carefully to avoid legal pitfalls while still acquiring the necessary information for their cases.

- **Evolving Legal Standards**: As financial markets evolve, so too do the laws that regulate them. New financial instruments and technologies, such as cryptocurrencies and peer-to-peer lending platforms, often create legal gray areas that can be difficult to interpret and apply.

- **Legal Defenses and Countermeasures**: Subjects of investigations often employ sophisticated legal strategies to challenge the evidence or the methods used by investigators. Staying informed about these potential defenses and preparing counter-strategies is crucial for successful prosecution.

To contextualize these concepts, consider a case study involving cross-border money laundering activities. A financial investigator based in Country A discovers evidence suggesting that a corporation is using a complex network of shell companies in Country B to launder money. The investigator must understand both countries' AML laws and work closely with legal and financial authorities in Country B to trace the funds, seize assets, and prosecute the individuals involved. This scenario illustrates the necessity of legal knowledge and international cooperation in tackling financial crimes effectively.

In conclusion, legal frameworks form the backbone of financial crime investigation. A thorough understanding of these laws, along with an appreciation of jurisdictional differences and the ability to navigate legal challenges, is essential for any financial investigator aiming to conduct effective and compliant investigations. This knowledge not only aids in the successful prosecution of crimes but also ensures the integrity and credibility of the investigative process itself.

Chapter 3: Preparing for Financial Investigations

Embarking on a career in financial investigation requires more than just an understanding of financial crimes and the tools used to detect them. Preparing for financial investigations involves a comprehensive approach that encompasses educational prerequisites, legal and ethical considerations, and the practical setup of an investigator's workspace. This chapter provides a structured guide to equipping aspiring financial investigators with the necessary foundation to embark on this demanding yet rewarding career path.

The preparation phase is crucial, as it sets the stage for the effectiveness and success of future investigations. This chapter will explore the key areas essential for any financial investigator to master before diving into active case work. Each section is designed to build a robust framework for the skills, knowledge, and ethical considerations that will guide investigators throughout their careers.

Understanding the educational pathways and background knowledge necessary for a career in financial investigation is the first step. This section will detail the degrees, certifications, and specific skill sets that are most beneficial for entering and excelling in this field. From degrees in finance, law, and criminology to certifications in fraud examination and financial forensics, we will explore how formal education and professional training contribute to a comprehensive understanding of both the theory and practice of financial investigation.

Financial investigators operate within strict legal and ethical boundaries. This section will examine the legal frameworks that guide the investigation process and the ethical dilemmas that can arise during investigations. Understanding these boundaries is crucial not only for conducting lawful and valid investigations but also for maintaining the integrity of the investigative process. Topics such as data protection laws, confidentiality obligations, and the ethical handling of sensitive information will be covered to ensure that investigators are prepared to handle the complexities of their role with professionalism and ethical clarity.

The practical aspects of preparing for financial investigations include setting up a workspace that supports efficient and secure investigative processes. This section will provide insights into the essential tools and technologies needed to create an effective office or field kit. From digital tools like encryption and secure communication software to physical setup recommendations that promote organization and efficiency, this part of the chapter will offer practical advice on creating a conducive working environment for financial investigations.

Additionally, this chapter will address how to build a professional network through associations and communities that can provide support, guidance, and continuous learning opportunities. Networking with other professionals can offer significant advantages, such as mentorship, partnership opportunities, and insights into industry best practices and emerging trends.

In summary, Chapter 3 serves as a comprehensive guide to preparing for a career in financial investigation. It ensures that aspiring investigators are not only well-informed about the educational and professional requirements but are also aware of the legal and ethical standards they must adhere to, and are equipped with the practical tools necessary for conducting effective investigations. This preparation is fundamental to developing a successful career in uncovering and combating financial crimes effectively.

3.1 Educational and Background Requirements

Embarking on a career as a financial investigator involves a blend of academic study, professional certifications, and real-world experience. This subchapter outlines the essential educational pathways and background knowledge necessary for aspiring financial investigators, providing a roadmap for those looking to enter and excel in this dynamic field.

Essential Degrees

The complexity of financial crimes requires a solid educational foundation in relevant fields. Here are some of the key degrees that can prepare individuals for a career in financial investigation:

- **Finance**: A degree in finance provides a strong understanding of financial markets, accounting principles, and financial management, all of which are crucial for analyzing financial records and understanding the nuances of financial transactions.

- **Criminology**: Studying criminology offers insights into the nature of crime, including the sociological and psychological aspects of criminal behavior, which can be particularly useful in understanding the motivations behind financial crimes.

- **Law**: A legal education can be invaluable, as it covers the statutes, regulations, and legal procedures that govern financial transactions and the prosecution of crimes.

- **Accounting**: A degree in accounting, especially with a focus on forensic accounting, equips individuals with the skills to examine financial records and identify discrepancies that may indicate fraudulent activities.

- **Computer Science or Information Technology**: As financial investigations increasingly involve digital data, a background in IT or computer science can be highly beneficial for understanding cybersecurity, data analysis, and the use of digital forensics tools.

Professional Certifications

In addition to academic degrees, professional certifications can enhance a financial investigator's credentials and demonstrate their specialized expertise to employers. Some of the most recognized certifications in the field include:

- **Certified Fraud Examiner (CFE)**: Offered by the Association of Certified Fraud Examiners, the CFE credential is recognized globally and equips professionals with knowledge in fraud prevention, detection, and deterrence.

- **Certified Financial Crime Specialist (CFCS)**: This certification covers a broad range of topics related to financial crime, including money laundering, fraud, compliance, and cybersecurity, providing a comprehensive skill set for tackling various financial crimes.

- **Certified Anti-Money Laundering Specialist (CAMS)**: CAMS certification is a standard in AML certifications and provides a deep understanding of anti-money laundering procedures.

- **Chartered Financial Analyst (CFA)**: Although primarily an investment management certification, the CFA program includes training on ethical and professional standards, which can be beneficial for financial investigators in understanding corporate finance and compliance issues.

Building Relevant Skills

Beyond formal education and certifications, financial investigators need a set of practical skills that are often honed through experience:

- **Analytical Skills**: The ability to analyze large amounts of data, recognize patterns, and draw logical conclusions is essential.

- **Attention to Detail**: Given the complexity of financial records and the subtlety of fraud schemes, a keen eye for detail is crucial.

- **Technical Proficiency**: Familiarity with forensic accounting software, data analysis tools, and cybersecurity measures is necessary as financial crimes become more technologically sophisticated.

- **Communication Skills**: Effective written and oral communication skills are essential for documenting findings, testifying in court, and explaining complex information to non-specialists.

- **Ethical Judgment**: Financial investigators must navigate ethical dilemmas and adhere to high ethical standards, as their work often involves sensitive financial information.

By integrating a solid educational foundation with professional certifications and practical skills, aspiring financial investigators can prepare themselves for a successful career in this challenging field. This preparation not only enhances their capability to conduct thorough investigations but also positions them as credible and competent professionals in the eyes of employers and peers.

3.2 Legal and Ethical Considerations

Navigating the complex legal and ethical landscape is a critical aspect of financial investigation. This subchapter discusses the crucial legal frameworks and ethical considerations that every financial investigator must understand and adhere to in order to conduct effective and lawful investigations. These elements ensure the integrity of the investigative process and safeguard the rights of all parties involved.

Understanding Legal Frameworks

Financial investigators must be well-versed in the specific laws and regulations that apply to their work. This includes both domestic and international legal frameworks that govern financial transactions, data privacy, and criminal procedures. Key areas include:

- **Anti-Money Laundering (AML) and Counter-Terrorism Financing (CTF) Laws**: These laws require financial institutions to implement systems to detect and report suspicious activities and ensure that they are not inadvertently used to launder money or finance terrorism.

- **Data Protection and Privacy Laws**: Given the sensitive nature of financial data, investigators must navigate various laws that protect personal information. Regulations such as the General Data

Protection Regulation (GDPR) in the European Union and the Health Insurance Portability and Accountability Act (HIPAA) in the United States set strict guidelines on data handling and privacy.

- **Fraud and Corruption Laws**: Understanding laws related to fraud, bribery, and corruption is essential for investigators working in sectors prone to these issues. This includes familiarization with statutes like the U.S. Foreign Corrupt Practices Act (FCPA) and the UK Bribery Act.

Ethical Considerations

The ethical dimension of financial investigation is just as critical as legal compliance. Financial investigators often deal with confidential and potentially damaging information, making ethical conduct essential. Important ethical considerations include:

- **Confidentiality**: Maintaining the confidentiality of information gathered during an investigation is paramount. Investigators must protect sensitive data from unauthorized access and disclosures, respecting privacy and the legal rights of subjects under investigation.

- **Impartiality**: Investigators must conduct their duties without bias, ensuring that their findings are based on evidence and not influenced by personal feelings or external pressures.

- **Transparency and Accountability**: When presenting findings, financial investigators should be transparent about their methods and findings. They should also be accountable for their actions, willing to face scrutiny and feedback regarding their investigative process.

- **Respecting Legal Rights**: Ensuring that the legal rights of those under investigation are respected is crucial. This includes adhering to laws that provide protections against unlawful search and seizure, and ensuring that all investigative actions are legally justified.

Handling Ethical Dilemmas

Financial investigators may occasionally face situations where legal and ethical paths seem to diverge. Handling these dilemmas requires a sound ethical framework and often, consultation with legal counsel or ethical advisors. Examples might include:

- Deciding whether to disclose information that could prevent a financial crime but might breach confidentiality agreements.
- Balancing the public interest with individual privacy rights when handling personally identifiable information in high-profile cases.

Practical Applications

To illustrate the application of these principles, consider a scenario where a financial investigator working for a corporation discovers evidence suggesting senior management is involved in creating false financial reports. The investigator must navigate complex ethical and legal terrain to report these findings. Ethical conduct would dictate that the investigator reports the misconduct despite potential internal pressures to suppress the information. Legally, the investigator must ensure the evidence is gathered and reported in compliance with applicable whistleblower laws and corporate policies.

In conclusion, understanding and adhering to legal and ethical frameworks is essential for conducting sound financial investigations. This not only ensures the legality and legitimacy of the investigative process but also upholds the professional integrity of the investigator and the trustworthiness of the financial institutions they represent. This subchapter has highlighted the importance of these considerations and provided guidelines for navigating the challenging scenarios that financial investigators frequently encounter.

3.3 Setting Up Your Workspace

For financial investigators, the environment in which they work can significantly impact their efficiency and effectiveness. This subchapter focuses on setting up a workspace that supports thorough investigations, ensuring that both office-based and field environments are equipped to handle the complexities of financial investigation. We'll cover the essential tools, security measures, and organizational strategies necessary to create a functional and secure workspace.

Essential Tools and Equipment

A well-equipped workspace is foundational for a financial investigator. The following tools and technologies are essential:
   - **Computers and Software**: High-performance computers with dual monitors can facilitate multitasking and complex analyses. Essential software includes advanced forensic tools, data analysis programs, and secure communication platforms.
   - **Secure Storage**: Financial investigators handle sensitive information that requires secure storage solutions. This includes both physical locking file cabinets for hard copy documents and encrypted digital storage solutions for electronic data.
   - **Specialized Investigative Tools**: Tools such as document scanners, shredders, and a

reliable multifunction printer are important for managing physical documents. Additionally, digital tools like blockchain analysis software or specialized accounting software are crucial for specific types of financial investigations.

Creating a Secure Workspace

Security is paramount in a financial investigator's workspace due to the confidential nature of the information involved. Here are key security measures to consider:

- **Physical Security**: Controlled access to the investigation area is necessary to prevent unauthorized entry. This can be managed through key card access systems and security cameras.
- **Data Security**: Implement robust cybersecurity measures, including firewalls, anti-virus software, and secure VPNs for network protection. Regular backups and encryption should be standard practice to safeguard data integrity and confidentiality.
- **Communication Security**: Use encrypted communication tools for sending and receiving sensitive information. Ensure that all conversations, whether via email, phone, or messaging apps, are secure and protected from interception.

Organizational Strategies

Efficiency in financial investigation often depends on how well the workspace is organized. Effective organizational strategies include:

- **Document Management Systems**: Implementing a document management system can help in organizing, storing, and retrieving documents efficiently. It should allow for easy indexing and searching of documents.

- **Task Management Tools**: Utilize project management software to track the progress of investigations, manage deadlines, and coordinate tasks among team members.

- **Regular Audits and Checks**: Conduct regular audits of both physical and digital workspaces to ensure compliance with security protocols and to identify any potential vulnerabilities.

Practical Application

Consider a scenario where a financial investigator is working on a complex case involving cross-border transactions suspected of money laundering. The investigator's office is equipped with high-specification computers that run powerful forensic software capable of analyzing large volumes of transaction data. The office is secured with access control systems, and all data is encrypted and backed up to secure servers. Communication with international law enforcement agencies is conducted through encrypted channels to maintain confidentiality and integrity.

The investigator uses project management software to outline the investigation's key stages, assign tasks to team members, and track the progress of each segment of the case. This organizational system allows the investigator to maintain a high level of oversight and ensure that no aspect of the case is overlooked.

Setting up an effective workspace is crucial for financial investigators. By ensuring that their environment is well-equipped, secure, and organized, investigators can enhance their ability to conduct thorough and successful financial investigations. This preparation not only facilitates the practical aspects of the job but also supports the overall success and integrity of the investigative process.

Chapter 4: Investigative Techniques and Approaches

In the realm of financial investigation, the methodology and rigor applied can significantly influence the outcome of a case. This chapter delves into the specialized investigative techniques and strategic approaches that are fundamental for effectively uncovering and analyzing financial crimes. Understanding these methods will equip financial investigators with the essential tools to navigate the complexities of their profession, from basic investigative tasks to applying sophisticated analysis and utilizing advanced technologies in their work.

The scope of this chapter spans various dimensions of financial investigative practices, each tailored to address the unique challenges posed by different types of financial crimes. Whether dealing with intricate money laundering schemes, corporate fraud, or complex tax evasion cases, the strategies discussed here provide a foundation for thorough, effective investigations.

Foundation of Investigative Techniques

Before delving into specific methods, it's essential to establish a fundamental understanding of what constitutes sound investigative practices. Financial investigations rely on a systematic approach to ensure that all relevant data is collected, analyzed, and interpreted accurately. This includes:

- **Documentation and Data Collection**: At the core of any financial investigation is the meticulous collection of all pertinent data. This ranges from financial statements and transaction logs to emails and other communication records. The ability to identify and gather the right data is crucial.

- **Interview Techniques**: Conducting interviews with potential witnesses or suspects is an art form that requires not only understanding the legal boundaries but also the ability to read people and extract the necessary information without coercion.

- **Analytical Review**: Once data is collected, the ability to analyze it to find inconsistencies, patterns, or anomalies is what sets apart skilled investigators. This involves both qualitative and quantitative analysis techniques.

Standard Investigative Techniques

This section explores the standard investigative techniques that form the backbone of financial investigation processes:

- **Document Analysis**: Critical in almost all financial investigations, this technique involves a detailed examination of financial documents to identify inaccuracies or peculiarities that may indicate fraud or other illegal activities.

- **Surveillance and Monitoring**: Often used in conjunction with other methods, surveillance can help verify the information gathered through other means or keep track of a suspect's activities.

- **Forensic Accounting**: This specialized area of accounting is used to reconstruct financial information when records are incomplete or purposely obfuscated. It's particularly useful in cases of embezzlement or corporate fraud.

Advanced Investigative Techniques

As financial crimes evolve, so too must the techniques used to investigate them. Advanced methods often leverage technology or novel approaches to tackle the challenges of modern financial crimes:

- **Digital Forensics**: In an era where much of our financial activity is conducted online, digital forensics is an essential tool. It involves the recovery and investigation of material found in digital devices, often pivotal in tracing the flow of illicit funds.

- **Cryptocurrency Tracing**: With the rise of digital currencies, understanding blockchain technology and being able to trace transactions on these platforms has become an invaluable skill for financial investigators.

- **Network Analysis**: Used to visualize relationships and transactions between entities, network analysis can reveal hidden connections and patterns among subjects involved in financial crimes.

Special Investigative Measures

Certain situations require measures beyond the standard investigative toolkit. These special measures, which may include legal instruments like subpoenas or warrants, are used when standard methods are insufficient:

- **Undercover Operations**: Sometimes, embedding an investigator within a targeted organization or group is necessary to gather firsthand information on illicit activities.

- **Wiretaps and Electronic Surveillance**: Authorized wiretapping can provide direct evidence and real-time data crucial in high-stakes investigations.

- **Asset Freezing and Seizure**: In cases where there is a significant risk of asset flight, preemptive measures such as freezing bank accounts or seizing properties can be critical to prevent the dissipation of ill-gotten gains.

Integrating Techniques for Comprehensive Investigations

Effective financial investigations often require a combination of these techniques. The integration of standard and advanced methods, tailored to the specifics of the case, ensures a thorough and robust investigation. For instance, a typical investigation might start with forensic accounting to identify anomalies and then employ digital forensics to track the flow of funds online, supplemented by interviews and surveillance to gather more contextual information.

Practical Applications and Case Studies

Throughout this chapter, practical applications and case studies will illustrate how these techniques are applied in real-world scenarios. These examples will provide insight into the decision-making process and the strategic thinking behind the choice and application of different investigative techniques. For instance, a case study might explore a multi-national bribery investigation involving the use of forensic accounting, digital forensics, and international cooperation.

In conclusion, this chapter will not only provide financial investigators with an understanding of the diverse tools and strategies available but also the knowledge of when and how to apply them effectively. By mastering these investigative techniques and approaches, investigators are better prepared to tackle the challenges they will face in the field, ensuring they can conduct their investigations with confidence and precision.

4.1 Standard Investigative Techniques

In the domain of financial investigation, mastery over standard investigative techniques is crucial. These foundational methods form the backbone of investigative work, enabling professionals to systematically gather evidence, analyze data, and establish factual bases for their cases. This subchapter provides a comprehensive look at the most commonly employed techniques in financial investigations, detailing their applications, strengths, and how they integrate into broader investigative strategies.

Document Analysis

Definition and Importance: Document analysis involves the systematic review of financial documents such as balance sheets, income statements, ledgers, and transaction records. This technique is crucial for identifying discrepancies, anomalies, or patterns that may suggest fraudulent activity or financial misconduct.

Application: Financial investigators start by securing all relevant documents, ensuring they are complete and authentic. The analysis might involve comparing documents against each other and against external data sources to validate their accuracy. Techniques such as ratio analysis, trend analysis, and cross-referencing are frequently used to detect signs of manipulation or irregularities.

Challenges: The primary challenge in document analysis is the volume of data and the potential for sophisticated concealment tactics by perpetrators. Increasingly, financial investigators need to be adept in using digital tools to manage and analyze large datasets effectively.

Interviews

Definition and Importance: Interviewing is a critical skill in financial investigations, used to gather information, corroborate facts, or gauge the credibility of suspects and witnesses. Effective interviewing can uncover insights that are not evident from documents alone.

Application: Preparation is key to successful interviewing. Investigators must be familiar with the case details and have specific objectives for each interview. Open-ended questions are often employed to elicit detailed responses, while more direct questions are used to confirm specifics or challenge inconsistencies. Interviews should be conducted in a controlled environment to ensure the comfort and cooperation of the interviewee.

Challenges: Challenges include dealing with uncooperative or hostile subjects and the potential for providing misleading information. Investigators must be skilled in behavioral analysis to detect deception and know how to navigate legal constraints surrounding interviews.

Surveillance and Monitoring

Definition and Importance: Surveillance involves observing subjects of interest to gather information about their behaviors, movements, and interactions. Monitoring typically refers to the ongoing observation of financial transactions or account activities to detect unusual or suspicious behavior.

Application: Surveillance can be physical, electronic, or a combination of both. Techniques might include following a subject, using video surveillance, or implementing electronic monitoring tools on financial transactions. In financial investigations, monitoring often focuses on real-time transaction data to flag anomalies immediately.

Challenges: Surveillance and monitoring must be conducted within the bounds of the law, respecting privacy rights and legal standards. Ethical considerations must be taken into account to avoid invasions of privacy, and specific legal permissions may be required for certain types of surveillance.

Forensic Accounting

Definition and Importance: Forensic accounting is the use of accounting techniques to uncover and investigate fraud and embezzlement within financial records. This discipline bridges the gap between accounting and law, providing the expertise to translate complex financial data into understandable, legally sustainable evidence.

Application: Forensic accountants examine financial data for signs of misstatements or inappropriate financial reporting. They employ techniques such as data mining and statistical analysis to reveal hidden patterns, fake accounts, or illicit transactions. Their findings can be crucial in legal proceedings, often serving as expert testimony.

Challenges: The complexity of financial systems and the cleverness of financial criminals can make forensic accounting particularly challenging. Forensic accountants must continually update their knowledge of accounting standards, fraud schemes, and technological advancements to stay effective.

Integration of Techniques

In practice, these techniques are rarely used in isolation. A financial investigator might begin with document analysis to identify potential areas of concern, use interviews to gather additional context or confirm details, employ surveillance to observe subject behavior, and apply forensic accounting to detail the financial discrepancies for legal proceedings. The integration of these techniques allows investigators to build a comprehensive, robust case against individuals or organizations involved in financial misconduct.

This subchapter has laid out the foundational techniques upon which financial investigations are built. Mastery of these methods empowers investigators to conduct thorough and effective investigations, ensuring they are well-prepared to tackle the complexities of financial crimes.

4.2 Advanced Investigative Techniques

As financial crimes evolve in complexity and sophistication, the tools and methods used to investigate these crimes must also advance. Advanced investigative techniques employ cutting-edge technology and innovative approaches to address the challenges presented by modern financial crime. This subchapter explores several advanced techniques that are crucial for financial investigators looking to stay ahead in their field.

Digital Forensics

Definition and Importance: Digital forensics involves the recovery and investigation of material found in digital devices, often to uncover data pertinent to financial crimes. As financial activities increasingly move online, the ability to analyze digital data effectively becomes critical.

Application: Digital forensics can be applied in numerous contexts, from recovering deleted emails that prove intent in a fraud case to tracing the origin of illicit online transactions. Techniques include data carving, which involves searching for and reconstructing raw data from storage media, and live analysis, which examines data on a running computer system.

Challenges: Challenges in digital forensics include the sheer volume of data and the speed at which digital technology evolves. Encryption and privacy-enhancing technologies also pose significant hurdles, requiring investigators to continually update their technical skills and tools.

Cryptocurrency Tracing

Definition and Importance: Cryptocurrency tracing involves analyzing transactions recorded on blockchain technologies to identify the flow of digital currencies that may be used for money laundering, financing terrorism, or other illicit activities.

Application: Using blockchain analysis tools, investigators can trace the movement of cryptocurrencies, identify wallet addresses, and sometimes link them to real-world identities. This process often involves mapping complex networks of transactions to detect patterns and relationships indicative of criminal behavior.

Challenges: The pseudonymous nature of cryptocurrencies and the global, decentralized ledger system present unique challenges. Moreover, the emergence of privacy coins and mixing services that obfuscate transaction trails requires advanced understanding and technologies to penetrate.

Network Analysis

Definition and Importance: Network analysis is used to visualize and analyze relationships and interactions between entities or individuals to uncover hidden structures and informants within financial networks.

Application: Financial investigators use network analysis to map out connections based on financial transactions, communication records, and other data points. This technique is particularly useful in large-scale fraud cases or complex schemes involving multiple parties and layered transactions.

Challenges: The complexity of financial networks and the dynamic nature of personal and business relationships can make network analysis intricate. Large datasets require powerful analytical tools and significant expertise to interpret accurately.

Behavioral Analysis

Definition and Importance: Behavioral analysis involves studying human behavior to predict or detect unusual or suspicious activities. It is often used in conjunction with other investigative techniques to provide a psychological perspective that may explain underlying motives or anticipate future actions.

Application: In financial investigations, behavioral analysis can help identify potential fraudsters by detecting patterns or anomalies in behavior, such as changes in spending habits or unusual interactions with certain accounts. This technique is also used during interviews to assess credibility and detect deception.

Challenges: Behavioral analysis requires a deep understanding of psychology and human behavior, and interpretations can be subjective. Additionally, cultural differences can affect behavior, complicating the analysis in international contexts.

Forensic Data Analytics

Definition and Importance: Forensic data analytics involves the use of statistical techniques to analyze complex datasets and identify anomalies that may indicate fraudulent activity or other financial crimes.

Application: This technique is widely used to sift through large volumes of transactional data to spot irregularities that warrant further investigation, such as duplicate payments, unusual transaction patterns, or inconsistencies in financial records.

Challenges: The volume and variety of data, along with the need for high computational power and sophisticated algorithms, pose significant challenges. Additionally, false positives can lead to unnecessary investigations, requiring careful calibration of analytical models.

Integration and Case Studies

To effectively combat financial crime, investigators often integrate multiple advanced techniques. For instance, a case involving international money laundering might utilize digital forensics to gather evidence from encrypted devices, cryptocurrency tracing to follow the money trail across borders, and network analysis to identify connections between suspects.

Case Study Example: In a real-world application, investigators might use digital forensics to recover deleted financial records from a suspect's computer. Following initial findings, cryptocurrency tracing could reveal transactions tied to illegal online marketplaces. Network analysis might then illustrate connections between the suspect and other parties involved in the scheme, while behavioral analysis during suspect interviews helps confirm suspicions or uncover additional leads.

This subchapter has outlined the advanced investigative techniques essential for modern financial investigators. By mastering these methods, professionals can enhance their ability to dissect sophisticated financial crimes, ensuring their skills remain effective and relevant in the rapidly evolving landscape of financial crime.

4.3 Special Investigative Measures

In the pursuit of combating sophisticated financial crimes, there are instances where conventional investigative techniques might not suffice. Special investigative measures, which often involve more intrusive methods, are sometimes required to effectively address and resolve high-stakes or complex cases. This subchapter explores the array of special investigative measures available to financial investigators, discussing their strategic applications, legal considerations, and the circumstances under which they are deployed.

Undercover Operations

Definition and Importance: Undercover operations involve investigators assuming false identities and roles to infiltrate organizations or groups suspected of financial wrongdoing. This method is particularly effective in gathering firsthand evidence and observing suspect activities without the usual filters that might be present in a more overt investigation.

Application: Financial investigators might pose as employees, business partners, or clients to get close to the subjects under scrutiny. The goal is to collect incriminating evidence directly from the inside, which can be pivotal for unraveling complex schemes like corporate fraud, insider trading, or money laundering within closed networks.

Challenges: The primary challenge of undercover operations is the risk they pose to the investigator's safety and the potential legal and ethical issues arising from interacting closely with suspects. Maintaining cover over extended periods can also be psychologically demanding.

Wiretaps and Electronic Surveillance

Definition and Importance: Wiretapping and electronic surveillance involve monitoring and recording telephone and digital communications. Authorized by legal warrants, these measures are crucial in gathering real-time data on suspects' activities and communications.

Application: In financial investigations, wiretaps can reveal conversations about illicit transactions, plans for committing financial crimes, or attempts to launder money. Electronic surveillance extends to emails, instant messages, and other digital communications, providing a comprehensive view of suspects' operations.

Challenges: The use of these techniques is heavily regulated to protect individuals' privacy rights. Investigators must obtain the necessary legal authorizations, typically requiring a demonstration of probable cause. There is also the risk of collecting vast amounts of irrelevant information, requiring significant resources to sift through.

Asset Freezing and Seizure

Definition and Importance: Asset freezing is a preventive measure used to prohibit the transfer, conversion, disposition, or movement of assets suspected to be derived from illegal activities. Asset seizure involves the legal process of confiscating these assets permanently.

Application: These measures are essential to prevent the dissipation of illicit gains, particularly in cases involving significant sums of money or other valuable assets. By freezing assets early in the investigation, investigators can safeguard these assets until the completion of legal proceedings.

Challenges: Asset freezing and seizure must be conducted with strict adherence to legal standards, often requiring detailed documentation and justification. Mistakenly freezing or seizing assets can lead to legal challenges and potential damages, underscoring the need for accuracy and thoroughness.

Special Court Orders

Definition and Importance: Special court orders, such as search warrants and subpoenas, are crucial tools that compel the production of evidence or authorize actions that would otherwise violate privacy rights. These orders are instrumental in accessing financial records, entering premises to conduct searches, or compelling individuals to testify or produce documents.

Application: Financial investigators use these legal instruments to gather critical evidence that cannot be obtained through less invasive means. For example, a subpoena may be necessary to acquire detailed banking records or transaction histories from financial institutions.

Challenges: Obtaining these orders requires presenting sufficient evidence to justify the need for such measures, often involving detailed preparatory work. Additionally, the execution of these orders must be meticulously planned to ensure compliance with legal requirements and to maximize the effectiveness of the search or seizure.

Integration of Special Measures in Investigations

Integrating these special measures requires careful planning and legal oversight. For instance, in a complex international fraud case, investigators might begin with standard document analysis and interviews. As evidence builds, they may escalate to wiretaps to capture real-time discussions of fraudulent schemes. Ultimately, asset freezing could be employed to prevent the transfer of stolen funds as the case nears prosecution.

Special investigative measures are powerful tools that, when used appropriately and legally, can significantly enhance the capabilities of financial investigators in tackling sophisticated and high-level financial crimes. However, the use of these measures requires a balanced approach to ensure that the investigation remains ethical, legal, and effective, maintaining the integrity of the investigative process and upholding the rights of all individuals involved.

Chapter 5: Advanced Investigative Strategies

In the dynamic and often intricate world of financial investigation, mastering advanced investigative strategies is crucial for addressing and dismantling sophisticated financial crimes. Chapter 5 delves into these complex strategies, exploring how financial investigators can elevate their approach to tackle elaborate schemes that go beyond ordinary fraud and money laundering cases. This chapter aims to provide investigators with a deep understanding of how to design and implement comprehensive investigation plans, utilize cutting-edge technology, and manage cases effectively to secure successful outcomes.

The foundation of any successful financial investigation is a well-crafted strategic plan. This plan serves as a roadmap, guiding investigators through the complexities of each case. It begins with defining clear objectives based on the initial assessment of the situation and then outlines the methodologies and resources necessary to achieve these goals. A strategic plan must be adaptable, allowing investigators to respond to new information and evolving circumstances without losing sight of the ultimate objectives.

As financial crimes become more technologically sophisticated, so too must the techniques used to investigate them. This section will cover the latest advancements in investigative technology, including artificial intelligence (AI), blockchain analysis, and data analytics platforms. These tools can dramatically enhance the ability of investigators to process large volumes of information, uncover hidden relationships, and predict fraudulent patterns before they fully manifest.

Effective case management is critical to the organization and execution of financial investigations. This involves coordinating teams, managing extensive documentation, and ensuring compliance with legal frameworks. Advanced case management strategies help in maintaining the integrity of the investigative process and ensuring that all procedural requirements are met, from evidence collection to the presentation of findings in court.

Financial crimes often transcend borders and jurisdictions, making collaboration and interagency cooperation indispensable. This section will explore strategies for building robust networks with other law enforcement agencies, international bodies, and private sector entities. Effective collaboration can provide access to a wider array of tools, expertise, and information, facilitating more comprehensive investigations and stronger legal cases.

Financial investigations can result in complex legal battles. Preparing for these challenges involves understanding the potential legal hurdles and planning strategies to overcome them. This includes meticulous documentation, the ethical handling of evidence, and the preparation of clear, compelling arguments to support the case in judicial settings.

The chapter will conclude by looking at innovative approaches that are setting new standards in the field of financial investigation. These include proactive surveillance techniques, predictive policing, and the use of cyber-forensics. Such innovations not only improve the effectiveness of investigations but also help in preempting financial crimes, setting new paradigms for security and compliance in the financial sector.

Through in-depth discussions and case studies, Chapter 5 will equip financial investigators with advanced strategies and insights needed to navigate the complexities of high-stakes investigations. It will serve as a guide for transforming challenges into opportunities to strengthen their investigative prowess and achieve significant professional milestones in the battle against financial crime.

5.1 Developing a Strategic Investigation Plan

The success of any financial investigation largely depends on the initial planning stages. A strategic investigation plan serves as the blueprint for the entire process, outlining the objectives, resources, methodologies, and milestones required to navigate complex financial inquiries. This subchapter explores the components of an effective strategic investigation plan, providing guidance on how to structure and implement these plans to maximize the efficiency and impact of financial investigations.

Identifying Objectives

The first step in developing a strategic investigation plan is to clearly define the objectives. Objectives should be specific, measurable, attainable, relevant, and time-bound (SMART). For a financial investigator, objectives could range from identifying the source of illicit funds, determining the methods used for money laundering, to establishing connections between suspected individuals and criminal organizations.

- **Specificity**: Objectives must be precise enough to guide the investigative actions. For example, rather than simply aiming to 'investigate fraud,' a specific objective would be 'to identify transactions that deviate from standard accounting practices by Q3.'

- **Measurability**: Each objective should have criteria that measure progress and success, such as 'collect and analyze 100% of financial transactions from the last two years.'

Resource Allocation

Effective resource allocation is crucial for the execution of the investigation plan. This includes determining the manpower, technology, and time required to achieve the objectives. Financial investigators must evaluate the availability of internal resources and the need for external assistance, such as legal advice, forensic accounting services, or specialized technological tools.

- **Human Resources**: Assigning roles and responsibilities based on the skills and expertise of team members ensures that all aspects of the investigation are covered by competent personnel.

- **Technological Resources**: Identifying the necessary technology for data analysis, surveillance, and record-keeping is essential. This may involve investing in new software or upgrading existing tools to handle complex data sets efficiently.

Methodological Approach

Choosing the right methodologies is critical for uncovering and documenting financial crimes effectively. This involves selecting investigative techniques that align with the objectives and legal requirements of the jurisdiction.

- **Document Analysis**: A thorough review of all financial documents and records to trace discrepancies and irregularities.
- **Interviews**: Structured and strategic interviews with key personnel and suspects to gather insights and corroborate data findings.
- **Forensic Analysis**: Employing forensic accounting techniques to reconstruct fraudulent transactions and identify hidden assets.
- **Digital Forensics**: Utilizing digital forensic tools to extract and analyze data from electronic devices, which can provide critical evidence in financial crime cases.

Milestones and Timeline

Setting clear milestones and a realistic timeline helps in tracking the progress of the investigation and ensuring that it remains on schedule. Milestones should be established for major phases of the investigation, such as completing the initial data collection, conducting key interviews, and finalizing the investigative report.

- **Initial Assessment**: Completing a preliminary review of the financial records within the first month.

- **Mid-Investigation Review**: Assessing progress at the halfway point to adjust the plan as necessary based on findings.

- **Final Analysis**: Concluding data analysis and beginning the compilation of the final report by the end of the investigation period.

Risk Assessment and Contingency Planning

Understanding potential risks and preparing for unforeseen complications are integral parts of strategic planning. Financial investigators should conduct a risk assessment to identify possible challenges that could derail the investigation, such as data integrity issues, non-cooperation from witnesses, or legal hurdles.

- **Contingency Plans**: Developing alternative strategies for overcoming significant obstacles, such as securing additional resources or employing different investigative techniques if initial methods prove ineffective.

By carefully crafting a strategic investigation plan, financial investigators can ensure that their approach is methodical, resource-efficient, and legally compliant. This foundational planning not only streamlines the investigative process but also enhances the likelihood of uncovering critical evidence and achieving substantive results.

5.2 Leveraging Technological Advancements

In the rapidly evolving landscape of financial crime, staying at the forefront of technological innovation is crucial for effective investigation. This subchapter explores how financial investigators can harness cutting-edge technologies to enhance their ability to detect, analyze, and resolve complex financial crimes. By integrating advanced tools and systems, investigators can gain a significant edge in uncovering illicit activities that are increasingly sophisticated and hidden within massive volumes of data.

The Role of Artificial Intelligence (AI)

Definition and Importance: Artificial Intelligence (AI) in financial investigations refers to the use of machine learning models and algorithms to predict, identify, and analyze patterns indicative of fraudulent activities. AI can process vast amounts of data at speeds and accuracies far beyond human capabilities.

Application: AI technologies are employed to automate the detection of anomalies in transaction data, identify unusual behavior patterns, and flag high-risk activities for further investigation. For example, AI can analyze historical transaction data to establish "normal" patterns and then monitor for deviations that may suggest fraudulent activities.

Challenges: While AI offers powerful capabilities, it also presents challenges such as the need for large datasets for effective training, the potential for bias in decision-making algorithms, and the requirement for continuous updates and oversight to adapt to new fraud tactics.

Blockchain Analysis

Definition and Importance: Blockchain technology is increasingly used in financial transactions, particularly with the rise of cryptocurrencies. Blockchain analysis involves examining blockchain ledgers to trace the movement of funds and identify the parties involved in transactions.

Application: Financial investigators use blockchain analysis tools to track the flow of cryptocurrencies in cases involving money laundering, ransomware payments, and other illicit uses of digital currencies. These tools can decode the complex web of transactions recorded on a blockchain and link them to real-world identities.

Challenges: The pseudonymous nature of blockchain can complicate the tracing process. Moreover, privacy-enhancing technologies like coin mixers can obscure the origins and destinations of funds, making it difficult to follow the money trail.

Advanced Data Analytics Platforms

Definition and Importance: Advanced data analytics platforms utilize a combination of statistical techniques, predictive modeling, and data visualization tools to interpret complex datasets. These platforms are crucial for uncovering hidden patterns and relationships within financial data.

Application: Investigators utilize these platforms to integrate and analyze data from various sources, including bank records, transaction logs, and external databases. By creating comprehensive visualizations, investigators can more easily communicate complex financial schemes and evidence to non-expert audiences, such as juries or regulatory bodies.

Challenges: The integration of disparate data sources can raise issues related to data compatibility and privacy. Additionally, the interpretation of complex analysis requires a high level of expertise to ensure accuracy and reliability.

Cyber Forensics Tools

Definition and Importance: Cyber forensics involves the examination of information in electronic formats, focusing on the recovery and investigation of data related to computer crime. Cyber forensics tools are essential for investigating fraud that involves digital devices and networks.

Application: These tools enable investigators to recover deleted, encrypted, or damaged files from suspects' devices, trace the origins of cyberattacks, and gather digital evidence that is admissible in court.

Challenges: Cyber forensics can be highly technical, requiring specialized knowledge in various software and hardware environments. The legal implications of digital evidence collection, including privacy concerns and the admissibility of evidence, also pose significant challenges.

Integrating Technology into Investigation Strategies

To fully leverage these technological advancements, financial investigators must integrate these tools into their broader investigation strategies. This integration involves training investigative teams, establishing protocols for technology use, and maintaining ethical standards in the deployment of powerful analytical tools.

Case Study Example: In a hypothetical scenario, a financial investigator might use AI to analyze discrepancies in financial statements, apply blockchain analysis to trace illicit cryptocurrency transactions, and employ cyber forensics to recover incriminating data from a suspect's computer. The convergence of these technologies provides a robust approach to dissecting and proving financial misconduct.

In conclusion, by embracing technological advancements, financial investigators can enhance their investigative capabilities, leading to more timely and accurate detection of financial crimes. The careful application of these technologies, coupled with a strong understanding of their limitations and challenges, is essential for modern financial investigations.

5.3 Case Management Techniques

Effective case management is essential for organizing, coordinating, and overseeing financial investigations. It ensures that each phase of the investigation is executed efficiently and that outcomes are thoroughly documented and legally compliant. This subchapter focuses on advanced case management techniques that can optimize the workflow of financial investigations, improve communication among team members, and enhance the overall quality of the investigative process.

Essential Components of Case Management

Organization of Information: Central to effective case management is the organization of vast amounts of data and documentation that financial investigations typically generate. This involves setting up a system where all information—be it digital data, paper documents, or communication logs—is stored in an accessible, secure, and orderly manner.

Task Delegation and Team Coordination: Proper delegation and coordination are crucial, especially in complex cases that might involve multiple investigators or teams. Clear assignment of roles and responsibilities, coupled with regular updates and team meetings, ensures that all team members are aligned and can collaborate effectively.

Timeline Management: Maintaining strict timelines is essential in financial investigations to ensure timely filing of legal proceedings, adherence to statutory deadlines, and efficient use of resources. Using project management tools can help track key milestones and deadlines.

Advanced Tools for Case Management

Project Management Software: Tools such as Asana, Trello, or Microsoft Project can facilitate the management of an investigation by allowing team members to track progress, assign tasks, and manage deadlines more efficiently. These tools also provide an overview of the project at a glance, which is crucial for managing complex cases with multiple moving parts.

Digital Evidence Management Systems: These systems are designed to handle the intake, storage, and analysis of digital evidence. They ensure that digital files are cataloged and searchable, maintaining the integrity and chain of custody of the evidence.

Communication Platforms: Secure communication platforms are essential for discussing sensitive case details. Encrypted messaging and email services ensure that internal communications are protected from unauthorized access, maintaining the confidentiality of the investigation.

Best Practices in Documentation and Reporting

Comprehensive Documentation: Every step of the investigation should be documented in detail. This includes keeping logs of decisions made, rationales for investigative paths taken, and summaries of findings. Comprehensive documentation is critical not only for the integrity of the investigation but also for legal proceedings that may follow.

Clear and Concise Reporting: The ability to synthesize complex information into clear, concise, and comprehensible reports is crucial. Financial investigators must ensure that their findings are presented in a manner that is understandable to non-experts, such as jurors or regulatory authorities.

Regular Review and Audits: Periodic reviews and audits of the case management process help identify any inefficiencies or areas for improvement. These reviews ensure that the investigation adheres to the highest standards of accuracy and legal compliance.

Integration of Case Management in Investigations

Effective case management should seamlessly integrate with the investigative process. For instance, as new evidence is uncovered or as certain lines of inquiry are pursued, case management systems should be updated in real-time to reflect these developments. This dynamic approach ensures that all team members are informed and that the investigation proceeds without delays.

Case Study Example: In a complex multi-national fraud investigation, an interagency team might use project management software to coordinate efforts across borders, employing digital evidence management systems to securely share findings. Regular video conferences and secure communications ensure that all team members, regardless of location, remain updated and engaged.

In conclusion, advanced case management techniques are indispensable for conducting thorough, efficient, and effective financial investigations. By leveraging modern tools and adhering to best practices in documentation and reporting, financial investigators can ensure that their investigations are well-organized, legally compliant, and successful in achieving their objectives.

Chapter 6: Working with Financial Institutions

In the intricate dance of financial investigation, financial institutions play a pivotal role as both arenas for financial crimes and allies in the fight against such activities. Understanding how to effectively collaborate with these institutions is essential for any financial investigator aiming to uncover and combat financial crimes. Chapter 6 delves into the nuances of working with banks, credit unions, investment firms, and other financial entities, providing investigators with the strategies and knowledge necessary to navigate this complex relationship.

Financial institutions often hold the key to unlocking the mysteries of financial crimes. They are the repositories of vast amounts of financial data, from transaction histories to account information, which are crucial in tracing illicit activities. Moreover, these institutions have regulatory obligations to report suspicious activities and implement anti-money laundering (AML) and counter-terrorism financing (CTF) measures. Thus, understanding how to access and utilize the information held by these institutions can significantly enhance the effectiveness of financial investigations.

This section will explore how investigators can forge and maintain effective partnerships with financial institutions. It will discuss the importance of establishing clear communication channels, understanding the regulatory environments within which these institutions operate, and respecting the legal constraints under which they function. By building trust and a mutual understanding of each party's roles and responsibilities, investigators can ensure quicker responses and more comprehensive support from these entities.

Working with financial institutions requires a thorough understanding of the legal frameworks governing the financial sector, including compliance regulations and privacy laws. Investigators need to be adept at navigating these regulations to access necessary information without infringing on privacy rights or breaching confidentiality agreements. This section will provide a detailed overview of these legal considerations, offering practical advice on how to effectively request and obtain pertinent information within the bounds of the law.

As financial transactions become increasingly digitized, the tools and technologies used to monitor and analyze these transactions are also evolving. This section will introduce the latest technological advancements that are transforming how financial institutions and investigators work together. From sophisticated data analytics platforms to blockchain analysis tools, understanding these technologies will allow investigators to more effectively track and analyze complex financial networks.

To illustrate the real-world application of the concepts discussed, this chapter will include case studies of successful collaborations between financial investigators and institutions. These case studies will highlight best practices, common challenges encountered, and innovative solutions employed to overcome these challenges.

Chapter 6 will equip financial investigators with the necessary tools and knowledge to effectively collaborate with financial institutions. By understanding how to work within the regulatory frameworks, leverage available technologies, and build effective partnerships, investigators can enhance their ability to uncover and tackle sophisticated financial crimes, making significant strides in the fight against economic crime.

6.1 Understanding Financial Systems

For financial investigators, a comprehensive understanding of how financial systems operate is crucial. These systems encompass the broad array of banking structures, investment firms, credit unions, and other financial services organizations that play pivotal roles in the global economy. This subchapter delves into the architecture of these systems, discusses the typical interactions between different types of financial institutions, and highlights the regulatory environments that govern their operations. Such knowledge is fundamental for investigators tasked with unraveling complex financial crimes.

Overview of Banking Systems

Banking Systems Structure: At its core, the banking system is a network of institutions licensed to accept deposits and make loans. Banks also provide other financial services, including wealth management, currency exchange, and safe deposit boxes. Understanding the hierarchy and function of various bank types—from major retail banks to specialized investment banks and private banks—is essential for navigating investigations.

Types of Financial Institutions:

- **Commercial Banks**: Handle deposits, loans, and basic investment products for the public and businesses.

- **Investment Banks**: Specialize in complex financial transactions such as mergers and acquisitions, underwriting, and issuing securities.

- **Credit Unions**: Member-owned institutions that provide traditional banking services but typically focus on smaller communities or specific employee groups.

- **Shadow Banks**: Non-bank financial intermediaries that provide services similar to traditional banks but outside normal banking regulations, such as hedge funds and private equity funds.

Understanding Financial Services

Range of Services: Financial services extend beyond traditional banking. They include investment services, insurance, and retirement planning. Each service area has its own set of rules and typical transactions, which may become relevant in various investigative scenarios.

Innovative Financial Products: Staying informed about new financial products and services, such as digital wallets, peer-to-peer lending platforms, and cryptocurrency exchanges, is crucial as these can often be exploited for money laundering and other illicit activities.

Regulatory Environment

Regulatory Frameworks: Financial institutions are heavily regulated to ensure stability and integrity within the financial system. Regulations cover a wide array, from the Bank Secrecy Act (BSA) in the United States, which requires financial institutions to assist government agencies in detecting and preventing money laundering, to the Basel Accords internationally, which set forth recommendations on banking laws and regulations.

Role of Regulatory Bodies:
- **Domestic**: Bodies like the Federal Reserve in the U.S., Financial Conduct Authority (FCA) in the UK, and others play critical roles in overseeing banking operations and compliance.
- **International**: Global frameworks and cooperation among international regulatory bodies help manage the complexities of cross-border finance and crime prevention.

Interactions and Data Sharing

Cooperation Among Institutions: Financial institutions often need to share information with one another to combat fraud and financial crimes, facilitated by legal frameworks that allow for such sharing under specific circumstances.

Public-Private Partnerships: These collaborations are essential for effective financial crime fighting. Examples include the Financial Action Task Force (FATF), which promotes legal, regulatory, and operational measures for fighting money laundering worldwide.

Challenges in Financial Systems Investigations

Complexity and Secrecy: Financial systems can be opaque, with a penchant for privacy that can border on secrecy, particularly in jurisdictions with strict privacy laws or in industries like private banking.

Technological Advancements: Rapid advancements in fintech present both opportunities and challenges for financial investigators, requiring continuous education and adaptation to new tools and methods.

By developing a deep understanding of financial systems, their regulatory environments, and the typical interactions between different financial institutions, investigators can enhance their ability to navigate complex financial landscapes. This foundational knowledge not only aids in identifying where financial crimes may occur but also in pinpointing how they can be detected and investigated within the bounds of the law.

6.2 Gathering Intelligence from Financial Institutions

Gathering intelligence effectively from financial institutions is a cornerstone of successful financial investigations. This subchapter focuses on the strategies and methodologies that financial investigators can use to extract critical data from banks, investment firms, and other financial entities. Understanding how to legally and efficiently gather this information can significantly enhance an investigator's ability to trace illicit activities and uncover complex financial schemes.

Establishing Legal Grounds for Information Gathering

Understanding Legal Permissions: Before gathering data, investigators must be well-versed in the legal frameworks that permit access to financial information. This includes knowing the specific conditions under which information can be requested, such as subpoenas, search warrants, or specific regulatory demands under financial oversight laws.

Compliance Requirements: Financial institutions are bound by laws like the Bank Secrecy Act (BSA), the Patriot Act in the U.S., and the General Data Protection Regulation (GDPR) in the EU, which dictate how they must handle requests for information. Investigators need to frame their requests in a way that aligns with these regulations to ensure compliance and cooperation.

Techniques for Effective Data Acquisition

Direct Requests: Often, the simplest approach to obtaining information is through direct requests to financial institutions. This requires clear communication and understanding of the type of data needed, why it is needed, and how it will be used, ensuring that requests are specific and legally justified.

Liaison with Compliance Departments: Building relationships with compliance officers within financial institutions can facilitate quicker and more effective data acquisition. Compliance professionals understand the intricacies of regulatory requirements and can assist in navigating the institution's protocols.

Use of Technology: Leveraging technology can streamline the process of data gathering. For instance, digital platforms that allow secure and compliant data sharing can reduce the turnaround time for information requests and improve the accuracy of the data received.

Analyzing Financial Data

Once data is acquired, the challenge shifts to analysis and interpretation. Financial investigators must be skilled in:

Transaction Analysis: Understanding the flow of funds through accounts, identifying unusual patterns, or transactions that do not fit the customer's usual business activities. This might involve the use of specialized software that can handle large volumes of transactions and apply filters for suspicious activities.

Link Analysis: Using data to map relationships between entities and individuals, which can reveal hidden networks involved in financial crimes. Software tools that visualize these connections can be invaluable in understanding the structure and scope of illicit activities.

Forensic Accounting: Employing forensic accounting techniques to trace illicit funds and uncover the origins and destinations of suspicious transactions. This often requires a detailed examination of financial records and may involve reconstructing incomplete or falsified accounts.

Challenges in Intelligence Gathering

Data Volume and Quality: Financial institutions often manage vast amounts of data, which can be overwhelming to process. Additionally, the quality of data can vary, requiring investigators to verify its accuracy and relevance.

Privacy Concerns: Balancing the need for information with respect to privacy laws is a constant challenge. Investigators must ensure that their methods of data gathering and analysis adhere to privacy laws and ethical standards.

International Cooperation: When financial crimes cross borders, investigators often need information from foreign institutions, which can complicate data gathering due to varying international laws and cooperation agreements.

Best Practices for Collaboration

To optimize the intelligence-gathering process, investigators should adhere to best practices that include:

Regular Training: Keeping abreast of the latest legal developments, technological advancements, and investigative techniques through ongoing training.

Establishing Protocols: Developing standardized protocols for requesting and handling data, which can improve efficiency and ensure consistency in investigations.

Enhancing Interagency Collaboration: Working closely with other regulatory bodies and law enforcement agencies to share knowledge, resources, and intelligence, thereby enhancing the overall effectiveness of financial investigations.

In conclusion, gathering intelligence from financial institutions requires a strategic approach that respects legal and regulatory boundaries while effectively leveraging available data. By mastering these strategies, financial investigators can significantly enhance their ability to uncover and prosecute financial crimes, ensuring the integrity and security of the financial system.

6.3 Building Relationships with Bank Compliance Officers and Other Insiders

Navigating the complexities of financial investigations often requires more than just understanding the legal and procedural landscapes—it demands establishing robust and effective relationships with key figures within financial institutions, particularly bank compliance officers. This subchapter discusses the strategic importance of building and maintaining these relationships, and provides practical guidance on how financial investigators can foster cooperation and mutual understanding with insiders who play pivotal roles in the regulation and oversight of financial activities.

The Role of Bank Compliance Officers

Understanding Their Role: Compliance officers in financial institutions are responsible for ensuring that their organizations adhere to all applicable laws, regulations, and internal policies. They are often the gatekeepers of significant amounts of sensitive financial data and possess an in-depth understanding of the institution's operations and the regulatory landscape.

Importance to Investigations: For financial investigators, compliance officers are invaluable allies who can provide insights into the institution's transactions, client behaviors, and potential red flags that might not be apparent from outside. Their cooperation can expedite access to crucial data and facilitate a deeper understanding of complex financial schemes.

Strategies for Engaging with Compliance Officers

Initial Contact and Relationship Building: Establishing a relationship with compliance officers should be approached with professionalism and respect for their expertise and responsibilities. Initial contacts should be formal, preferably through official channels, and should clearly communicate the purpose and scope of the inquiry.

Maintaining Open Lines of Communication: Regular communication is key to fostering trust and cooperation. Keeping compliance officers informed about the progress of investigations and any developments that might impact their institution helps reinforce the partnership and ensures ongoing collaboration.

Providing Feedback: Sharing results from the investigation that relate to the institution's operations can be beneficial. It not only underscores the value of the compliance officer's assistance but can also help the institution enhance its own compliance measures and fraud prevention strategies.

Navigating Challenges and Building Trust

Confidentiality and Discretion: Compliance officers are bound by strict confidentiality obligations. Financial investigators must respect these constraints by ensuring that any information shared is handled discreetly and securely.

Legal and Regulatory Constraints: Understanding the legal boundaries within which compliance officers operate is crucial. Investigators should ensure that their requests for information are always compliant with regulatory requirements, helping avoid putting compliance officers in difficult positions.

Mutual Educational Opportunities: Inviting compliance officers to training sessions or workshops on financial crimes can be mutually beneficial. These sessions provide compliance personnel with insights into investigative processes and techniques, while investigators learn about the latest compliance challenges and solutions.

Leveraging Relationships for Better Outcomes

Case Study Analysis: Demonstrating through case studies how collaborative efforts have led to successful identification and prosecution of financial crimes can serve as powerful examples of the benefits of these relationships.

Strategic Alliances: Beyond individual cases, strategic alliances between investigative bodies and financial institutions can be formalized to facilitate regular exchanges of information, training, and resources, enhancing the capabilities of both parties to detect and prevent financial crimes.

Recognition and Respect: Acknowledging the contributions of compliance officers and respecting their professional limitations strengthens relationships and fosters a cooperative environment that is conducive to effective investigations.

In conclusion, building and maintaining strong relationships with bank compliance officers and other insiders is critical for effective financial investigations. These relationships not only facilitate quicker access to vital information but also ensure that investigations are conducted within the bounds of legal and regulatory frameworks. By respecting the roles, responsibilities, and expertise of these insiders, financial investigators can significantly enhance their ability to uncover and combat financial crimes.

Chapter 7: International and Multi-jurisdictional Investigations

In today's interconnected world, financial crimes frequently transcend national borders, posing unique challenges that require cooperation across various jurisdictions. Chapter 7 delves into the complexities of international and multi-jurisdictional financial investigations. This chapter aims to equip financial investigators with the necessary knowledge and strategies to effectively navigate the challenges posed by global financial crimes. By exploring international laws, cooperation frameworks, and practical approaches to cross-border investigations, this chapter provides a comprehensive guide for tackling crimes that span multiple countries.

Financial crimes on an international scale often involve sophisticated schemes such as offshore banking fraud, international money laundering, and global tax evasion. These crimes exploit differences in legal systems, regulatory environments, and enforcement capacities, making their investigation and prosecution exceedingly complex. Understanding the scope and mechanisms of these crimes is crucial for developing effective strategies to combat them.

This section will introduce the international legal and regulatory frameworks that govern financial crimes across borders. Key international agreements, such as those facilitated by the United Nations Office on Drugs and Crime (UNODC) and the Financial Action Task Force (FATF), play critical roles in setting standards and fostering cooperation among countries. Understanding these frameworks is essential for ensuring that investigations comply with international laws and benefit from global cooperation.

Navigating the challenges of multi-jurisdictional investigations involves dealing with diverse legal systems, language barriers, cultural differences, and varying levels of law enforcement capability. This section will discuss these challenges in detail and offer strategies for overcoming them, such as leveraging international legal assistance treaties and engaging with international law enforcement agencies like INTERPOL.

Effective tools and techniques are essential for managing the complexities of international financial investigations. This includes the use of international data exchange platforms, collaborative investigative teams, and advanced technological tools for tracking financial transactions across borders. Practical guidance on utilizing these tools will be provided to enhance the investigator's ability to gather evidence and pursue leads internationally.

To illustrate the real-world application of concepts discussed in this chapter, detailed case studies of successful international financial investigations will be presented. These case studies will highlight best practices, innovative solutions, and lessons learned from actual investigations, providing valuable insights that can be applied in future cases.

Chapter 7 aims to provide financial investigators with a deep understanding of the intricacies involved in international and multi-jurisdictional financial investigations. By mastering the legal frameworks, embracing international cooperation, and effectively utilizing advanced investigative tools, financial investigators will be better equipped to tackle the global challenges of financial crimes, ensuring the integrity of financial systems worldwide.

7.1 Challenges of Global Financial Crime

Global financial crime presents a series of unique challenges that complicate the efforts of financial investigators to detect, track, and prosecute offenders across borders. This subchapter explores these challenges in depth, providing insights into the complexities of navigating international laws, the difficulties posed by jurisdictional variances, and the logistical hurdles inherent in global investigations.

Legal and Jurisdictional Complexities

Varying Legal Standards: One of the most significant challenges in international financial investigations is the diversity in legal frameworks across different countries. What constitutes a crime in one country might be legal in another, and vice versa. Additionally, procedural differences in how investigations must be conducted can vary widely, which can complicate cross-border collaboration.

Extradition Issues: Extradition—the process of delivering a person from one jurisdiction to another for prosecution or punishment—is fraught with difficulties. Extradition treaties between countries may not always exist, and even when they do, political, humanitarian, or legalistic reasons can delay or prevent extradition.

Cultural and Language Barriers

Communication Difficulties: Effective communication is crucial for the success of any investigation, but in the international arena, language barriers can significantly hinder this process. Misunderstandings or misinterpretations can lead to errors in the investigation or legal processes.

Cultural Differences: Cultural norms and practices can influence business operations and legal perceptions, leading to varied interpretations of what might constitute suspicious activity. These differences require investigators to be culturally aware and sensitive to ensure that their actions are both respectful and effective.

Technological and Data-Sharing Obstacles

Inconsistent Data Protection Laws: Data protection regulations, such as the GDPR in the European Union, impose strict rules on the transfer and processing of personal data. These laws can restrict the sharing of information critical to investigations, complicating international cooperation.

Lack of Compatible Technology: Differences in technological infrastructure and capabilities between countries can hinder the sharing and analysis of financial data. In some cases, incompatible systems can delay or prevent the efficient exchange of information necessary for tracking financial transactions across borders.

Operational and Logistical Challenges

Resource Limitations: Conducting investigations that span multiple countries often requires significant resources, which may not always be available. Financial constraints, limited personnel, and insufficient technological tools can impede the progress of international investigations.

Time Zone Differences: Simple logistical issues such as coordinating communication across different time zones can complicate timely decision-making and slow down the investigative process.

Strategies for Overcoming International Challenges

To address these challenges, investigators can adopt several strategies:

Building International Networks: Developing relationships with international law enforcement, regulatory bodies, and financial institutions can facilitate smoother cooperation and information sharing.

Leveraging International Legal Instruments: Utilizing tools such as mutual legal assistance treaties (MLATs) and memoranda of understanding can provide formal channels for data exchange and collaborative efforts.

Training and Cross-cultural Education: Providing investigators with training on international laws and cultural practices can enhance their ability to operate effectively across different jurisdictions.

Investing in Technology: Adopting advanced technologies that can securely and efficiently handle data across borders is crucial. Cloud-based platforms and blockchain technology offer potential solutions for some of the data-sharing challenges.

By understanding and addressing these diverse challenges, financial investigators can enhance their effectiveness in the global arena, ensuring that they are equipped to tackle the complexities of international financial crime. This subchapter not only outlines the hurdles but also provides practical advice on navigating these obstacles, thereby empowering investigators to conduct more successful global financial investigations.

7.2 Building International Cooperation

Effective international cooperation is pivotal for addressing the increasingly global nature of financial crimes. This subchapter explores the mechanisms and strategies for fostering collaboration among countries, international agencies, and global financial institutions. It highlights the benefits of such cooperation and provides practical guidance on establishing and maintaining effective international partnerships to combat financial crimes more effectively.

Importance of International Cooperation

Shared Challenges: Financial crimes often involve complex networks that operate across multiple countries, exploiting the gaps and weaknesses in national regulatory systems. By cooperating internationally, countries can pool resources, share critical information, and leverage collective expertise to tackle these sophisticated crimes.

Enhanced Effectiveness: International cooperation allows for a more comprehensive approach to enforcement and prosecution. It ensures that criminals cannot evade justice merely by crossing borders, and it helps to dismantle transnational criminal organizations by attacking them from multiple angles.

Frameworks for International Cooperation

Bilateral and Multilateral Agreements: Countries often enter into bilateral (between two countries) or multilateral (involving several countries) agreements specifically designed to improve cooperation in law enforcement efforts, including those targeting financial crimes. These agreements can provide a framework for sharing investigative resources and intelligence.

Role of International Organizations: Several international organizations play crucial roles in fostering global cooperation against financial crimes. These include:

- **Financial Action Task Force (FATF)**: An intergovernmental body that sets international standards for combating money laundering, terrorist financing, and other related threats.

- **INTERPOL**: Provides a range of policing capabilities to enhance the ability of member countries to fight crime including financial crime.

- **World Bank and International Monetary Fund (IMF)**: Provide technical assistance and funding for projects aimed at improving financial systems and enhancing regulatory frameworks in member countries.

Techniques for Effective Collaboration

Joint Investigation Teams (JITs): JITs involve officials from two or more countries forming a team to conduct investigations within one or more of the involved countries under a shared legal framework. This approach is particularly effective for complex cases that require coordinated, simultaneous action.

Information Sharing Platforms: Developing secure digital platforms for information sharing can significantly enhance the effectiveness of international cooperation. Such platforms allow for real-time data exchange and can support joint analyses and investigations.

Training and Capacity Building: Conducting joint training sessions and workshops can help standardize investigative techniques and foster mutual understanding among international partners. These initiatives also build capacity by equipping teams with the latest skills and technologies needed to combat modern financial crimes.

Challenges and Solutions in International Cooperation

Legal and Cultural Differences: Differences in legal systems and cultural norms can pose significant barriers to effective cooperation. To mitigate these challenges, it's essential to develop a deep understanding of these differences and work towards harmonizing approaches where possible.

Privacy and Data Protection Laws: Stringent data protection laws in some countries can restrict the sharing of information. Navigating these laws requires careful legal planning and, in some cases, the establishment of agreements that respect the privacy laws of all parties involved.

Political Will and Trust: Building and maintaining political will and trust is essential for effective international cooperation. This can be achieved through regular communication, transparency in operations, and shared success stories that highlight the benefits of collaboration.

To illustrate the practical application of these concepts, this subchapter will include case studies of successful international financial investigations. These examples will showcase how different cooperation mechanisms were utilized and the outcomes that were achieved, providing valuable lessons and insights for future cooperative efforts.

In conclusion, building robust international cooperation is critical for effectively combating the global dimensions of financial crime. By understanding and leveraging the various frameworks, techniques, and strategies for international collaboration, financial investigators can enhance their capacity to tackle these complex crimes across borders.

7.3 Using Technology to Bridge Gaps

As financial crimes become increasingly complex and globally interconnected, leveraging technology is essential for bridging the gaps in international and multi-jurisdictional investigations. This subchapter explores the various technological tools and platforms that enable more efficient data sharing, communication, and collaboration across borders, enhancing the capability of financial investigators to tackle financial crimes on a global scale.

Key Technological Tools

Digital Forensics Tools: These tools are crucial for analyzing electronic data involved in financial crimes, especially when the data spans multiple jurisdictions. Digital forensics can recover deleted files, decrypt encrypted data, and trace electronic transactions, providing evidence that is critical in prosecuting financial crimes.

Blockchain Technology: Given its inherent characteristics of decentralization, transparency, and immutability, blockchain technology is increasingly used for secure and traceable transactions. For investigators, blockchain analytics tools can trace and visualize cryptocurrency transactions, helping to identify the flow of illicit funds across the globe.

Big Data Analytics: Big data technologies allow for the handling and analysis of vast amounts of data from various sources, including banking transactions, communication records, and social media platforms. These tools use advanced algorithms and machine learning to detect patterns, trends, and anomalies indicative of financial crimes.

Enhancing Communication and Collaboration

Secure Communication Platforms: In an era where data breaches and cyber threats are prevalent, secure communication platforms are vital for ensuring that sensitive information exchanged between international agencies remains confidential. These platforms often employ end-to-end encryption to safeguard data integrity and privacy.

Cloud-Based Collaboration Tools: Cloud technology facilitates real-time collaboration and information sharing among international teams. These tools can host documents, databases, and software applications in a centralized, accessible environment, enabling teams from different jurisdictions to work together seamlessly.

Virtual Private Networks (VPNs): VPNs create secure connections over the internet, allowing investigators to access and share resources safely across networks. This is particularly useful for accessing restricted information or conducting investigations discreetly.

Overcoming Technological Challenges

Interoperability: One of the major challenges in using technology across different jurisdictions is the lack of interoperability between systems. Standardizing data formats and protocols can help mitigate this issue, ensuring that systems can communicate and exchange information smoothly.

Data Privacy and Security: Different countries have varying regulations concerning data privacy and security. Navigating these laws requires a careful approach to ensure compliance while still leveraging the benefits of technological tools. Regular audits and adherence to international data protection standards can help address these concerns.

Training and Capacity Building: Keeping up with rapidly evolving technology requires ongoing training and capacity building for financial investigators. Establishing regular training programs and workshops that focus on the latest technological tools and their applications in financial investigations can enhance the efficacy and efficiency of international collaborations.

Case Studies and Best Practices

This subchapter will include detailed case studies that illustrate successful applications of technology in international financial investigations. These real-world examples will showcase the practical use of digital forensics, blockchain analytics, and big data in uncovering and prosecuting financial crimes. Additionally, best practices derived from these case studies will provide guidelines on effectively integrating technology into investigation strategies.

In conclusion, using technology to bridge gaps in international financial investigations presents both opportunities and challenges. By understanding and implementing the right tools, financial investigators can enhance their ability to conduct thorough and effective investigations across borders, adapting to the digital age of financial crime.

Chapter 8: Communication and Reporting

Effective communication and accurate reporting are critical components in the realm of financial investigation. This chapter delves into the various aspects of how financial investigators can enhance their communication strategies and refine their reporting techniques to ensure clarity, compliance, and impact. It is essential for investigators to articulate complex financial data and investigation findings in a way that is understandable and persuasive to a range of audiences, including legal teams, regulatory bodies, and, potentially, a jury.

Bridging Complexity and Comprehension: Financial investigations often involve intricate details and complex terminologies that can be challenging for non-specialists to understand. Effective communication skills help in demystifying these complexities and presenting information in a clear, concise manner.

Building Interdisciplinary Teams: Financial investigations typically require a collaborative approach, involving experts from various fields such as law, finance, and technology. Effective communication fosters a productive working environment, ensuring that all team members are aligned and informed.

Engaging Stakeholders: Whether it's updating senior management, liaising with law enforcement, or communicating with regulatory bodies, the ability to convey information effectively is crucial. This includes being able to tailor the communication style and content according to the audience's needs and expectations.

Advanced Reporting Techniques

Structured Reporting Frameworks: This section will introduce structured frameworks and guidelines for creating reports that are not only comprehensive but also easy to navigate and understand. Emphasis will be placed on organizing information in a logical flow, using visual aids such as charts and graphs, and highlighting key findings in an executive summary.

Legal and Procedural Compliance: Reports must adhere to legal and procedural standards, particularly when they are to be used in judicial or regulatory proceedings. This includes ensuring that all claims are substantiated with evidence, that the report maintains objectivity, and that it respects confidentiality and privacy laws.

Technological Tools for Reporting: Leveraging modern technology can greatly enhance the reporting process. This can include the use of data visualization tools, advanced document editing software, and secure sharing platforms that ensure the integrity and confidentiality of the report.

Communication Skills Development

Training and Workshops: To enhance communication skills, financial investigators can benefit from specialized training sessions and workshops that focus on public speaking, technical writing, and interpersonal communication.

Feedback and Continuous Improvement: Regular feedback from peers, supervisors, and audience members can provide valuable insights into how communication and reporting can be improved. Encouraging a culture of continuous improvement can lead to more effective communication strategies over time.

Case Management and Documentation

Systematic Documentation: Keeping thorough and organized records throughout the investigation is crucial for effective communication and reporting. This section will cover best practices for documenting investigative processes, decisions, and findings in a way that they can be easily referenced and utilized in reports.

Integrating Findings into Reports: How investigators can effectively integrate their findings into reports will be explored, including techniques for ensuring that data supports the narrative and that any conclusions drawn are logically presented and well-substantiated.

This chapter will include practical examples and case studies to illustrate how effective communication and advanced reporting techniques have been applied successfully in real-world financial investigations. These examples will showcase different scenarios, from internal corporate investigations to public inquiries and criminal prosecutions, providing readers with a diverse range of contexts and solutions.

Chapter 8 aims to equip financial investigators with the essential communication and reporting skills needed to effectively convey complex information and ensure their findings have the desired impact. By mastering these skills, investigators can enhance their professionalism and efficacy, making significant contributions to their fields and ensuring that their investigative insights lead to appropriate actions and resolutions.

8.1 Effective Communication Skills

Effective communication is a fundamental skill for financial investigators, enabling them to articulate complex information clearly and persuasively across a variety of contexts and audiences. This subchapter explores the various aspects of effective communication, including verbal, written, and non-verbal skills, and provides practical guidance on how financial investigators can enhance their communication effectiveness to achieve better outcomes in their investigations.

Importance of Communication in Financial Investigations

Communication skills are crucial at every stage of a financial investigation—from gathering information and interviewing witnesses to presenting findings to colleagues, supervisors, regulatory bodies, or in court. Effective communication ensures that complex financial data is understood by non-specialists, facilitates collaboration across diverse teams, and aids in presenting a compelling narrative to support the investigator's conclusions.

Verbal Communication Skills

Clarity and Precision: In verbal communications, it is essential to be clear and precise. Financial investigators must articulate complex information in a manner that is easily understandable, avoiding jargon when communicating with non-experts. This often involves breaking down complex concepts into simpler terms and using analogies that make the information more relatable.

Active Listening: Effective communication is not just about speaking but also listening. Active listening involves fully concentrating on what is being said rather than just passively hearing the message of the speaker. This skill is particularly important during interviews and meetings where understanding nuances and underlying meanings can provide critical insights.

Assertiveness: Financial investigators often need to assert their points without being aggressive. Assertiveness involves expressing thoughts and feelings in a direct, honest, and respectful way. It is crucial when dealing with non-cooperative witnesses or in negotiations.

Written Communication Skills

Structured Writing: Good written communication in financial investigations is structured, concise, and well-organized. Reports should start with an executive summary that outlines key findings and conclusions, followed by detailed sections that present the evidence and analysis supporting these conclusions.

Use of Visual Aids: Incorporating charts, graphs, and tables can enhance the clarity of written communications, making complex data more accessible and easier to understand. Visual aids can help summarize large volumes of data succinctly and highlight key trends or anomalies.

Proofreading and Editing: Ensuring that written communications are free from errors and easy to read is vital. Proofreading and editing are critical processes that help improve the quality of a report, making it more professional and credible.

Non-Verbal Communication Skills

Body Language: In face-to-face communications, non-verbal cues such as eye contact, facial expressions, posture, and gestures play a significant role in conveying confidence and credibility. Being aware of and controlling these signals can reinforce the verbal message.

Professional Appearance: The way a financial investigator presents themselves can also communicate professionalism and credibility. A neat and professional appearance can positively influence how messages are received, particularly in formal or legal settings.

Enhancing Communication through Technology

Telecommunication Tools: With the increasing use of virtual meetings and interviews, mastering telecommunication tools has become essential. Financial investigators should be proficient in using various online platforms and ensure they can manage the technical aspects of virtual communication effectively.

Presentation Software: Tools like PowerPoint or Prezi can be used to create impactful presentations that reinforce verbal communications. Learning how to use these tools effectively can greatly enhance the delivery of findings in meetings or conferences.

Communication Challenges and Solutions

Dealing with Difficult Conversations: Financial investigators often face challenging conversations, particularly when delivering bad news or confronting unethical behavior. Preparing for these conversations, staying calm, and focusing on facts rather than emotions can help manage such situations effectively.

Cultural Sensitivity: In a globalized work environment, being culturally sensitive is crucial. This includes understanding and respecting cultural differences in communication styles and adapting accordingly to avoid misunderstandings.

Practical Applications and Case Studies

This subchapter will also present case studies demonstrating successful communication strategies employed in financial investigations. These real-life examples will illustrate how overcoming communication barriers, effective report writing, and skilled verbal delivery have directly contributed to successful investigative outcomes.

In conclusion, developing and honing communication skills can significantly enhance the effectiveness of financial investigators. By mastering both the art and science of communication, investigators can ensure that their findings are not just heard but understood and acted upon, thereby making a decisive impact on their professional fields.

8.2 Writing Detailed Reports

In the field of financial investigation, the ability to produce detailed, clear, and compelling reports is essential. These reports serve not only as a record of the investigation but also as the primary means of communicating findings to stakeholders, regulatory bodies, and courts. This subchapter provides a comprehensive guide to writing effective investigative reports in financial investigations, highlighting the structure, content, and techniques that ensure these documents are both informative and persuasive.

The Importance of Effective Reporting

Documentation of Evidence: Reports in financial investigations document the evidence gathered, ensuring that there is a permanent record that can be referred back to at any stage. This is crucial for maintaining the integrity of the investigation and for legal proceedings.

Communication with Stakeholders: Well-written reports communicate the findings of the investigation clearly to stakeholders who may not have a background in finance or law, such as company executives, regulators, or jurors. The clarity of these reports can significantly impact the decision-making processes.

Legal and Regulatory Compliance: In many cases, the style and format of reports will need to comply with specific legal and regulatory requirements. Ensuring adherence to these requirements is vital for the acceptance and usefulness of the report.

Components of an Effective Investigation Report

Executive Summary: This section provides a concise overview of the report, including the background of the investigation, key findings, conclusions, and recommendations. The executive summary should be clear enough that a reader can understand the essence of the report without reading the full document.

Introduction: The introduction should set the scene for the investigation. It includes the objectives of the investigation, the allegations or issues being addressed, and a brief description of the investigative methodology used.

Methodology: This section details the methods and procedures used in the investigation, explaining how evidence was collected and analyzed. It should provide enough detail to allow the reader to understand the process and assess the thoroughness of the investigation.

Findings: The findings section is the core of the report. It should present the evidence collected, organized logically by issue or by the sequence of the investigation. Each finding should be supported by specific evidence, and the relevance of the evidence to the investigation's objectives should be clearly explained.

Conclusions and Recommendations: Based on the findings, this section draws conclusions about the issues investigated. It should also provide recommendations for actions to be taken in response to the findings, such as changes to procedures, disciplinary actions, or further investigations.

Appendices: Supporting materials, such as full financial data, detailed analysis, relevant documents, and a list of interviewees, should be included in the appendices to provide additional context or evidence without cluttering the main body of the report.

Techniques for Effective Report Writing

Clarity and Precision: Use clear and precise language to ensure that the report is understandable to those without specialist knowledge. Avoid jargon and technical terms where possible, or provide explanations for necessary terms.

Logical Structure: Organize information in a logical order that guides the reader through the investigation. Use headings and subheadings to break up the text and guide the reader's understanding.

Use of Visuals: Incorporate charts, graphs, and tables to illustrate key points and trends. Visual aids can help to summarize complex information and make it more accessible.

Objective Tone: Maintain an objective and neutral tone throughout the report. Avoid speculative language and clearly distinguish between findings supported by evidence and those based on assumptions.

Common Pitfalls and How to Avoid Them

Overwhelming Detail: Avoid overwhelming the reader with excessive detail. Focus on including information that is relevant to the objectives of the investigation and the decisions that need to be made based on the report.

Bias: Be vigilant for any unconscious bias in how information is presented. Ensure that all conclusions are firmly based on evidence and that all reasonable interpretations of the evidence are considered.

Inconsistencies: Ensure consistency in terms of terminology, formatting, and presentation. Inconsistencies can confuse the reader and undermine the credibility of the report.

Practical Applications and Case Studies

This subchapter will include practical examples and case studies that highlight successful reporting in complex financial investigations. These examples will demonstrate how the principles and techniques discussed have been applied in real-world scenarios, providing valuable lessons on what works and what does not in investigative reporting.

In conclusion, mastering the art of report writing is essential for financial investigators. Detailed, clear, and well-structured reports not only facilitate effective communication of complex information but also ensure that the findings of financial investigations lead to appropriate and informed actions.

8.3 Handling the Media

In high-profile financial investigations, dealing with media interest is often inevitable. Effective media handling can protect the integrity of the investigation, manage public perception, and even aid in gathering more information. This subchapter delves into strategies for managing media relations in financial investigations, providing guidelines for engaging with journalists, controlling the flow of information, and using media attention to support investigative goals.

Understanding the Role of Media in Financial Investigations

Public Interest: Financial crimes, especially those involving large sums of money or prominent companies, can attract significant public interest. Media coverage can shape public perception of the investigation and the entities involved.

Accountability: Media scrutiny can also serve as a check on the conduct of both the investigators and the organizations under investigation, promoting transparency and accountability.

Influence on Proceedings: Media reports can influence the proceedings of an investigation by shaping public opinion, which in turn can impact regulatory or legal actions and decisions.

Developing a Media Strategy

Designating a Spokesperson: Appoint a trained spokesperson or a team responsible for all media interactions. This person should have a deep understanding of the investigation's details and the implications of disclosing certain information.

Proactive vs. Reactive Approach: Decide whether to take a proactive approach, issuing press releases and holding press conferences, or a reactive approach, responding to media inquiries as they arise. The chosen approach should align with the overall goals of the investigation and the legal constraints involved.

Consistent Messaging: Ensure that all communications with the media are consistent and aligned with the facts of the investigation. Consistency helps to maintain credibility and control over the narrative.

Engaging with the Media

Press Releases: Use press releases to provide clear, concise, and factual information about the investigation. This can help set the narrative and reduce misreporting.

Press Conferences: In cases with significant media attention, holding a press conference can be an effective way to address multiple media queries at once and clarify complex issues directly.

Interviews: Selective engagement in interviews can be used to discuss the investigation more deeply, clarify misunderstandings, or highlight important aspects of the case not covered in written communications.

Legal and Ethical Considerations

Confidentiality: Be aware of the legal boundaries concerning what information can be publicly disclosed. Ensure that all communications comply with confidentiality agreements, privacy laws, and regulatory guidelines.

Impartiality: Avoid making statements that could be perceived as prejudicial or biased, which could affect the outcomes of ongoing investigations or subsequent legal proceedings.

Accuracy: Double-check all information for accuracy before it is released to the media to avoid any potential harm that could result from the dissemination of incorrect data.

Managing Crisis Situations

Crisis Communication Plan: Have a crisis communication plan in place to address potential negative publicity or misinformation that may arise during the investigation. This plan should include steps for quick response and strategies for rectifying incorrect or damaging information.

Monitoring Media Coverage: Regularly monitor media coverage to understand public perception and the effectiveness of the media strategy. This can inform adjustments to the approach as the investigation progresses.

Engagement with Legal Teams: Coordinate closely with legal advisors to ensure that all public communications are vetted for potential legal implications, especially during critical phases of the investigation.

Leveraging Media for Investigative Purposes

Public Assistance: Sometimes, appealing to the public through the media can aid an investigation, such as in cases where witnesses are encouraged to come forward with information.

Deterrence: Publicizing enforcement actions and the progress of investigations can deter potential financial crimes and encourage compliance with regulatory standards.

Practical Applications and Case Studies

This subchapter will include case studies illustrating successful media handling in high-profile financial investigations. These will demonstrate how effective media strategies supported the goals of the investigation, managed public perception, and maintained the integrity of the process.

In conclusion, handling media relations is a critical aspect of conducting financial investigations, especially those attracting public or international interest. Effective media engagement requires careful planning, strategic communication, and adherence to legal and ethical standards. By implementing the strategies discussed, financial investigators can manage media interactions proficiently, ensuring that public communications bolster rather than hinder the investigative process.

Chapter 9: Building a Network of Trust

In an era characterized by rapid globalization and digital transformation, the ability to forge, sustain, and leverage trust within networks has become an indispensable asset. Trust is not merely a soft skill or a moral attribute; it is a strategic imperative that underpins the effectiveness of personal interactions, organizational collaborations, and international partnerships. Chapter 9, "Building a Network of Trust," is meticulously crafted to guide you through the multifaceted process of building and nurturing trust across various networking spheres—each demanding a unique approach and understanding.

Trust is the invisible architecture upon which professional networks are built. It influences decisions, drives collaborations, and affects how information is shared and received. A network devoid of trust is merely a collection of contacts without depth or value. In contrast, a trust-rich network is a dynamic, resilient entity capable of driving real change and facilitating success. It is no longer sufficient to network solely for the sake of expanding one's list of contacts; one must strategically cultivate these relationships based on mutual respect, shared goals, and, most importantly, trust.

The initial section of this chapter dives deep into the essence of establishing trustworthy connections. Here, we discuss the significance of trust in professional environments, highlighting how vital reliable networks are to career and business success. According to a LinkedIn survey, approximately 80% of professionals attribute their career progression to robust networking. This statistic underscores the importance of trust in these relationships, as it is often the glue that holds networks together during times of uncertainty and change.

Building and maintaining trust involves more than just occasional interactions; it requires a consistent and deliberate effort characterized by honesty, integrity, and transparency. This part of the chapter provides practical techniques for nurturing trust, such as maintaining open lines of communication, meeting commitments, and handling conflicts constructively. Additionally, we delve into the role of emotional intelligence in understanding and managing interpersonal relationships, which is crucial for long-lasting trust.

To bring theoretical concepts to life, this section examines various case studies that illustrate successful trust-based collaborations. From multinational corporations to small non-profit organizations, these examples reveal how entities leverage trust to overcome challenges and achieve collective goals.

Moving beyond individual and corporate settings, the second section of the chapter explores inter-agency collaboration. In today's interconnected world, the ability to effectively collaborate with other agencies—be they governmental, private, or non-profit—is essential for addressing complex challenges that no single entity can manage alone.

Effective cooperation requires a foundational level of trust, without which efforts can quickly become mired in bureaucracy and inefficiency. This segment discusses strategies for fostering inter-agency trust, including developing shared goals, establishing clear communication protocols, and implementing joint projects. These strategies are designed to create a cohesive working environment that promotes shared success.

In an age where data breaches are increasingly common, the secure sharing of information is a critical aspect of trust between agencies. We explore cutting-edge technologies and protocols that safeguard sensitive information, ensuring that trust is not compromised by external threats.

This part highlights the multifaceted benefits of inter-agency collaboration, such as improved resource efficiency, enhanced problem-solving capabilities, and increased innovation through the integration of diverse perspectives. Furthermore, these efforts often lead to stronger advocacy and more comprehensive service delivery, bolstering public trust in the participating organizations.

The final section of the chapter addresses the complexities of international networks, where trust must bridge not only geographical distances but also cultural differences.

Here, we discuss the myriad benefits of international cooperation, from accessing global markets to exchanging cultural and professional insights. These advantages are critical for businesses looking to expand internationally and for governments striving to enhance diplomatic relations.

Building international contacts involves more than just understanding different business practices; it requires an appreciation of cultural nuances and the ability to adapt one's approach accordingly. This section offers strategies for effectively communicating and maintaining relationships across cultures, ensuring that these international networks are both robust and productive.

Finally, we tackle the challenge of cultural differences, providing practical advice for navigating complex international waters. This includes training in cultural competency, the use of cultural liaisons, and strategies for fostering an atmosphere of mutual respect and understanding.

In summary, Chapter 9 serves as a comprehensive guide to building a network of trust across local, national, and international levels. Through a blend of insightful theories, practical strategies, and real-world examples, this chapter equips you with the tools necessary to navigate and succeed in today's interconnected, trust-dependent world.

9.1 Establishing Trustworthy Connections

In the intricate tapestry of professional relationships, trust is the thread that holds everything together. Establishing trustworthy connections is not only foundational to career success but also essential for personal growth and organizational development. This subchapter explores the crucial elements of building reliable networks, where trust acts as a driving force that facilitates both personal and collective advancements.

The value of a well-connected, trustworthy network in today's competitive environment cannot be overstated. Networks provide access to new opportunities, critical resources, timely information, and support during professional challenges. They are not merely transactional but are fundamental to career longevity and success. In reliable networks, trust ensures that members are willing to share openly, advocate for each other, and provide mutual support, thereby creating a fertile ground for reciprocal benefits.

Studies consistently show that professionals with robust networks are better positioned for promotions, job opportunities, and business ventures. For instance, a study by the Harvard Business Review highlighted that individuals with diverse and reliable contacts are more innovative and tend to have higher performance ratings in their careers. Such networks act as echo chambers for sharing industry insights, trends, and strategic information, which are invaluable for staying ahead in any field.

Building trust within a network requires intentional actions and consistent behavior. This section outlines several key techniques that professionals can employ to establish and maintain trust within their networks.

Consistency in one's professional interactions and transparency in communications are fundamental to building trust. When people act in predictable, reliable ways, it reduces uncertainty and builds confidence in their intentions and capabilities. Transparent communication helps in setting clear expectations and reducing misunderstandings, which are crucial for maintaining long-term relationships.

Integrity involves adhering to a set of ethical principles and being honest in all professional dealings. When individuals demonstrate integrity, they earn the respect and trust of their peers. Closely linked to integrity is accountability; owning up to one's actions, especially when things go wrong, is vital for sustaining trust.

Emotional intelligence—the ability to understand and manage one's emotions and the emotions of others—plays a critical role in building trust. It enables individuals to navigate complex interpersonal dynamics, empathize with others, and engage in meaningful interactions. High emotional intelligence can lead to deeper and more trusting relationships as it fosters a supportive and understanding network environment.

To illustrate the power of trust in professional networks, this section delves into various case studies from both the corporate world and non-profit sectors.

In the corporate sector, trust is often a decisive factor in successful partnerships and joint ventures. For example, a case study involving two leading technology firms shows how trust enabled them to share resources and collaborate on a groundbreaking new product. Despite the competitive risks, their shared trust led to a successful market launch and substantial mutual benefits.

In the non-profit sector, trust plays a pivotal role in forming alliances and coalitions that address social issues. A case study of a global health initiative reveals how diverse organizations, spanning different countries and cultures, built a trust-based network to combat a widespread health crisis effectively. Their success was heavily dependent on the trust established through years of collaboration and shared goals.

In conclusion, Section 9.1 underscores the undeniable importance of trust in building professional networks. By employing key techniques and learning from real-world examples, professionals can enhance their ability to establish and maintain trustworthy connections, paving the way for a more successful and fulfilling career. This exploration not only provides practical insights but also inspires readers to actively engage in and prioritize trust-building in their professional endeavors.

9.2 Inter-agency Collaboration

In today's increasingly interconnected professional landscape, the ability to collaborate effectively across agency boundaries is not just advantageous—it's imperative. Inter-agency collaboration harnesses the collective strengths of diverse organizations, leading to enhanced problem-solving capabilities, innovation, and resource efficiency. This subchapter delves into the strategies necessary for fostering effective collaboration between agencies, the importance of sharing information securely, and the wide-ranging benefits that such collaborative efforts can yield.

Effective inter-agency collaboration hinges on several foundational strategies that ensure all parties involved can work together efficiently and productively. These strategies are designed to mitigate the common pitfalls of collaborative efforts, such as miscommunication, resource duplication, and goal misalignment.

The first step in successful inter-agency collaboration is to define and agree upon common goals. These objectives should address the core reasons for the collaboration and be aligned with the strategic interests of all participating entities. Establishing clear, mutual goals not only provides a shared focus but also enhances motivation among the partners.

Communication is the lifeline of any collaborative effort. Establishing structured communication channels ensures that information flows efficiently between agencies. Regular meetings, shared digital platforms, and clear points of contact are essential components of effective communication frameworks. These channels help maintain transparency, facilitate quick decision-making, and keep all parties informed of progress and challenges.

To maximize the effectiveness of inter-agency collaborations, implementing joint protocols for project management, data sharing, and conflict resolution is crucial. These protocols standardize procedures and responses across the board, reducing uncertainty and smoothing out the operational aspects of collaborative projects.

As agencies increasingly rely on digital tools and data sharing, securing sensitive information becomes paramount. The integrity of data and the privacy of stakeholders involved are non-negotiable aspects that require robust security measures.

Utilizing advanced data protection technologies such as encryption, secure access controls, and blockchain can significantly enhance the security of shared information. These technologies help prevent unauthorized access and ensure that data integrity is maintained throughout the collaboration process.

Conducting regular security audits and reviews of the data-sharing processes helps identify vulnerabilities and reinforce data protection strategies. These audits ensure compliance with relevant data protection laws and build trust among the collaborating agencies, crucial for sustaining long-term partnerships.

The collaborative efforts between agencies are not without their challenges, but the benefits they bring often outweigh the complexities involved. These benefits can be substantial, ranging from enhanced efficiency to broader societal impacts.

By pooling resources, agencies can achieve more significant results with less expenditure, reducing redundancy and leveraging each agency's strengths. This synergy not only drives cost efficiency but also amplifies the impact of the collaborative efforts.

Collaboration brings diverse perspectives and expertise to the table, greatly enhancing the problem-solving capabilities of the involved parties. This diversity fosters creative solutions and innovative approaches to complex challenges that might stump a single agency.

Joint efforts often result in stronger advocacy when addressing issues of public concern. By presenting a united front, agencies can exert more substantial influence on policy decisions and public opinion, leading to more effective implementation of solutions and broader impact.

In conclusion, Subchapter 9.2 outlines the critical strategies and benefits of inter-agency collaboration. By focusing on effective communication, shared goals, and secure data practices, agencies can forge powerful alliances that transcend traditional boundaries and drive collective success. The insights provided here serve as a blueprint for agencies looking to enhance their collaborative efforts and achieve greater outcomes through partnership.

9.3 International Networks

The globalized nature of today's business environment necessitates strong international networks that transcend national borders and cultural boundaries. Building and maintaining such networks are crucial for organizations aiming to leverage global opportunities and navigate the complexities of international markets. This subchapter explores the strategic importance of international cooperation, techniques for building and utilizing international contacts effectively, and best practices for managing cultural differences within global networks.

International cooperation offers a plethora of strategic advantages that are essential for organizations looking to expand their footprint globally. These benefits not only include increased market reach but also access to a diverse pool of talent, innovative ideas, and potential cost efficiencies.

Expanding into international markets offers businesses the opportunity to increase their customer base and revenue streams. International networks provide the local insights and partnerships necessary to navigate new markets effectively, reducing the risks associated with international expansion.

International networks foster collaboration across borders, leading to innovation through the blending of diverse ideas and practices. Such collaborations can result in unique product offerings and solutions tailored to meet the needs of global consumers.

International networks open up access to a global talent pool, bringing diverse skills and perspectives that enhance the organizational capability. Additionally, these networks can facilitate cost-effective sourcing of materials and resources from different parts of the world, optimizing supply chains and production processes.

Building international contacts is an art that requires strategic planning and execution. Here, we discuss several key approaches to establishing and maintaining effective international relationships.

Identifying and connecting with key influencers and decision-makers in relevant industries globally is crucial. Attending international conferences, participating in global trade shows, and joining international business forums are effective ways to expand professional networks.

Technology plays a critical role in maintaining international connections. Utilizing platforms like LinkedIn, industry-specific forums, and virtual meeting tools helps keep the communication lines open and ensures continuous engagement with international contacts.

Regular engagement with international contacts is vital to keep relationships active. This can be achieved through frequent communications, collaborative projects, and mutual visits. Such ongoing interactions strengthen ties and foster a sense of community and belonging among network members.

Effectively managing cultural differences is critical to the success of international networks. Cultural misunderstandings can lead to conflicts and miscommunications, which can undermine trust and cooperation.

Cultivating a deep understanding of the cultural norms, values, and business practices of different regions is essential. Organizations can benefit from cultural training programs that educate employees about the nuances of interacting with international colleagues and partners.

Adapting communication styles to fit the cultural expectations of international partners is crucial. This may involve adjusting the formality of language, communication preferences (such as email versus phone calls), and meeting etiquette to align with cultural norms.

Respecting cultural differences and approaching them with openness and curiosity fosters mutual respect. Emphasizing inclusivity and valuing diverse perspectives within international networks enhances collaboration and trust.

In conclusion, Subchapter 9.3 highlights the significant benefits of fostering robust international networks and provides a framework for successfully building and managing these relationships. By embracing cultural diversity and leveraging global connections, organizations can achieve a competitive edge in the international arena, driving growth and innovation on a global scale. This subchapter serves as a guide for businesses and professionals seeking to harness the full potential of their international networks.

Chapter 10: Future Trends and Career Advancement

As we move further into the 21st century, the field of financial investigation is evolving at an unprecedented pace. New technologies, emerging financial markets, and evolving regulatory landscapes are shaping the future of financial crime investigation. Chapter 10 explores these dynamics, offering a forward-looking perspective on the trends that will influence the field and providing guidance on how financial investigators can advance their careers in this changing environment.

Technological Advancements: This chapter examines how emerging technologies such as artificial intelligence (AI), blockchain, and big data analytics are transforming financial investigations. It discusses the opportunities these technologies present for more effective tracking and analysis of financial transactions and the challenges they pose, such as increased complexity and new types of cybercrimes.

Globalization of Financial Markets: As financial markets become more interconnected, financial crimes are increasingly transnational in nature. This section will explore how financial investigators can adapt to the global nature of modern financial crimes and the skills required to handle investigations that span multiple jurisdictions.

Regulatory Changes: With financial markets evolving rapidly, regulatory frameworks are constantly being updated to close loopholes and address new challenges. This chapter will discuss the impact of these regulatory changes on financial investigations and how investigators can stay ahead of the curve by understanding and anticipating these developments.

Career Advancement in Financial Investigation

Skill Development: To keep pace with the evolving field, financial investigators must continually develop their skills. This section provides a roadmap for ongoing professional development, including advanced certifications, specialized training, and higher education opportunities that can enhance an investigator's expertise and marketability.

Networking and Professional Associations: Building a professional network is crucial for career advancement. This chapter highlights the importance of connecting with peers, mentors, and industry leaders through professional associations, conferences, and seminars. It discusses how these connections can provide valuable insights, career advice, and opportunities for collaboration.

Specialization Opportunities: As the field of financial investigation becomes more complex, there is a growing need for specialists in areas such as cybersecurity, forensic accounting, and compliance. This section explores the various specialization paths available and how they can position an investigator for leadership roles and other advanced positions.

Future Challenges and Innovations

Adapting to Change: The ability to adapt to rapid changes is a critical skill for future financial investigators. This chapter discusses strategies for staying flexible and responsive to new challenges, including maintaining a proactive learning mindset and staying informed about industry trends.

Ethical Considerations: As financial investigations become more technologically driven and globally integrated, ethical considerations are increasingly at the forefront. This section examines the ethical dilemmas that financial investigators might face and provides guidance on maintaining integrity and ethical standards in complex and high-stakes environments.

Innovative Practices: Finally, this chapter looks at innovative practices that are setting new standards in the field of financial investigation. From predictive analytics to collaborative international task forces, these innovations are not just shaping current practices but also paving the way for the future of financial investigations.

Chapter 10 aims to equip financial investigators with a comprehensive understanding of the future landscape of their profession. By exploring emerging trends, discussing strategies for career advancement, and providing insights into future challenges, this chapter prepares investigators to not only adapt but thrive in the ever-evolving world of financial investigation.

10.1 Navigating Emerging Trends in Financial Crime

As financial markets expand and technology advances, the landscape of financial crime continues to evolve, presenting new challenges and opportunities for financial investigators. This subchapter delves into the emerging trends in financial crime, highlighting how these changes are reshaping the field and offering insights into how investigators can adapt to stay ahead.

Technological Advancements and Financial Crime

Artificial Intelligence (AI) and Machine Learning: AI and machine learning are revolutionizing the way financial transactions are monitored and analyzed. These technologies can identify patterns and anomalies in vast datasets much faster and more accurately than human analysts. For investigators, this means quicker detection of potential financial crimes and more efficient allocation of investigative resources. However, criminals are also leveraging AI to devise more sophisticated schemes, necessitating a higher level of technical expertise for investigators.

Blockchain and Cryptocurrencies: The rise of cryptocurrencies and blockchain technology has introduced a new frontier in financial transactions, which are decentralized and often anonymized. While blockchain provides opportunities for transparent and secure transactions, it also poses significant challenges for financial investigators due to the difficulties in tracing illicit flows of cryptocurrency. Understanding blockchain forensics is becoming increasingly important for investigators dealing with money laundering, ransomware attacks, and other cyber-enabled financial crimes.

Cybersecurity Threats: As financial systems become more digitized, cybersecurity breaches have become a more common vector for financial crimes. Data breaches can expose sensitive financial information, leading to large-scale fraud and identity theft. Financial investigators must now possess a strong foundation in cybersecurity principles and collaborate closely with IT security experts to address these threats effectively.

Globalization of Financial Systems

Cross-border Transactions: Globalization has increased the volume and complexity of cross-border financial transactions. This integration of global financial markets presents unique challenges for investigators, such as dealing with multiple regulatory environments and different legal systems. Financial investigators must develop expertise in international finance laws and foster relationships with international agencies to effectively track and investigate transnational financial crimes.

Offshore Financial Centers: Offshore jurisdictions and tax havens complicate the tracking and prosecution of financial crimes. Investigators need to navigate the legal and logistical challenges posed by jurisdictions with strict secrecy laws and varying degrees of cooperation with international law enforcement.

Regulatory Changes and Compliance

Evolving Legal Frameworks: Financial regulations are continually updated to address new types of financial crimes and close loopholes in existing legislation. Investigators must stay informed about these changes to ensure compliance in their investigative practices and to understand the legal boundaries within which they operate.

Anti-Money Laundering (AML) and Counter-Terrorism Financing (CTF) Laws: The global standard for AML and CTF is constantly being refined. Financial investigators must keep abreast of these changes, particularly the recommendations set forth by the Financial Action Task Force (FATF), which influence domestic legislation and international cooperation.

Future Threats and Opportunities

Emerging Financial Technologies (FinTech): Innovations in FinTech, such as peer-to-peer platforms, mobile banking, and digital wallets, are reshaping financial services. While these developments offer convenience and efficiency, they also create new avenues for fraudsters and financial criminals. Investigators must understand these technologies to effectively monitor and safeguard against potential abuses.

Big Data and Analytics: The use of big data in financial services offers tremendous potential for detecting and analyzing trends in financial crime. Harnessing this data requires sophisticated analytical tools and techniques, such as predictive analytics, which can forecast potential fraudulent activities based on historical data and trends.

In conclusion, the field of financial investigation is undergoing rapid transformations due to technological advancements, globalization, and evolving regulatory landscapes. To navigate these changes effectively, financial investigators must continuously develop their technical expertise, understand international financial systems, and adapt to regulatory changes. By staying informed and adaptable, investigators can not only keep pace with emerging trends in financial crime but also leverage these developments to enhance their investigative strategies.

10.2 Career Advancement in Financial Investigation

The field of financial investigation offers a myriad of pathways for career advancement, reflecting its dynamic nature and the growing complexity of financial crimes. This subchapter explores how financial investigators can elevate their careers by enhancing their skills, expanding their professional network, and specializing in high-demand areas of expertise. Each aspect is crucial for staying relevant in an ever-evolving industry and for moving into leadership roles within the field.

Enhancing Professional Skills

Continuous Learning: The first step in career advancement is the commitment to lifelong learning. Financial investigators must keep pace with the latest investigative techniques, regulatory changes, and technological advancements. This can be achieved through advanced certifications, continuing education courses, and seminars.

- **Certifications**: Certifications such as Certified Fraud Examiner (CFE), Certified Financial Crime Specialist (CFCS), and Certified Anti-Money Laundering Specialist (CAMS) provide recognition of professional expertise and commitment to the field. These credentials can open doors to new opportunities and are often sought after by employers.

- **Advanced Degrees**: Pursuing higher education, such as a Master's degree in Forensic Accounting, Law, Business Administration, or

Cybersecurity, can significantly enhance an investigator's knowledge base and open up higher-level positions that require advanced qualifications.

Technical Proficiency: As financial crimes increasingly involve sophisticated technologies, proficiency in digital tools, data analytics platforms, and cybersecurity measures is essential. Investigators should seek training in these areas to handle complex cases involving cyber elements and high volumes of digital data.

Expanding Professional Networks

Industry Associations: Joining professional associations related to financial investigation, such as the Association of Certified Fraud Examiners (ACFE) or the International Association of Financial Crimes Investigators (IAFCI), can provide valuable resources, including training, networking opportunities, and industry insights.

- **Networking Events**: Regular participation in workshops, conferences, and seminars not only aids in continuous education but also helps in building a professional network. Networking can lead to mentorship opportunities, partnerships, and even job offers.

- **Online Communities**: Engaging in online forums and professional social media groups can also expand an investigator's network beyond geographic limits, providing access to a global community of experts.

Specializing in High-Demand Areas

Choosing a Specialty: As financial crimes diversify, there is a growing need for investigators specialized in areas such as cryptocurrency, international money laundering, corporate espionage, and regulatory compliance. Specializing in one of these areas can make an investigator particularly valuable to organizations dealing with specific types of financial risks.

- **Cyber-Financial Investigations**: With the increase in cybercrimes, specializing in cyber-financial investigations can position an investigator at the intersection of cybersecurity and financial crimes, dealing with issues like ransomware, online fraud, and identity theft.

- **Regulatory Compliance**: Specialists in regulatory compliance are essential for organizations navigating the complex landscape of global financial regulations. This role involves ensuring that businesses operate within legal frameworks, making it critical as regulations continue to evolve.

Building a Personal Brand

Industry Contributions: Writing articles, participating in speaking engagements, and contributing to professional publications can help establish an investigator as a thought leader in the field.

Teaching and Mentoring: Sharing knowledge through teaching courses or mentoring younger professionals can also enhance an investigator's reputation and provide personal satisfaction.

Visibility in Professional Circles: Active participation in professional circles, including leading sessions at industry conferences and participating in panel discussions, raises an investigator's profile and demonstrates their expertise to peers and potential employers.

Navigating Challenges and Seizing Opportunities

Adaptability: The ability to adapt to new challenges and rapidly changing environments is crucial for advancement. This includes willingness to take on new responsibilities, learn new skills, and occasionally, make career moves that might involve risks but offer greater rewards.

Ethical Leadership: As investigators climb the career ladder, it becomes increasingly important to uphold and advocate for high ethical standards. Leadership roles require not just expertise, but integrity, fairness, and a commitment to justice.

Career advancement in financial investigation requires a proactive approach to skill enhancement, networking, and specialization. By embracing continuous learning, building a robust professional network, and specializing in areas of high demand, financial investigators can significantly enhance their career prospects. This proactive and strategic approach ensures that investigators not only adapt to the changing landscape of financial crime but also lead the way in developing more effective investigation practices and shaping the future of the industry.

10.3 Innovations in Financial Investigation

The landscape of financial investigation is constantly evolving, driven by rapid technological advancements, changing regulatory environments, and the increasing complexity of global financial systems. Innovations in technology, methodology, and interdisciplinary approaches are shaping the future of financial investigations. This subchapter explores these innovations, examining how they are being integrated into practice and how they are transforming the field to better tackle modern financial crimes.

Technological Innovations

Artificial Intelligence (AI) and Machine Learning: AI is revolutionizing financial investigations by automating complex processes such as data analysis and pattern recognition. Machine learning models can predict fraudulent activities by analyzing trends and anomalies in vast datasets, significantly reducing the time investigators need to identify suspicious activities. These technologies are particularly effective in areas like anti-money laundering (AML) and transaction monitoring.

Blockchain Forensics: As cryptocurrencies and blockchain technologies become more mainstream, the need for advanced forensic techniques to track and analyze blockchain transactions has grown. Tools like blockchain explorers and specialized analytics platforms are being developed to trace the flow of cryptocurrencies in illegal activities, providing transparent and immutable evidence that can be crucial in legal proceedings.

Big Data Analytics: The use of big data in financial investigations allows for the processing and analysis of unstructured data from diverse sources such as social media, financial logs, and internet activity records. Advanced analytics platforms are capable of integrating this information to create comprehensive profiles and behavioral patterns that help in identifying and preventing fraud.

Methodological Innovations

Behavioral Analysis Techniques: Understanding the psychological and behavioral patterns that underlie financial crimes can enhance investigative methods. Techniques from behavioral economics and psychology are increasingly being applied to predict and detect fraudulent behavior, offering insights that go beyond traditional financial records analysis.

Predictive Analytics: This approach involves using statistical models and forecasting techniques to identify the likelihood of future events based on historical data. In financial investigations, predictive analytics can be used to flag high-risk transactions or potential fraud before they occur, enabling proactive rather than reactive measures.

Geospatial Analysis: Integrating geographic information systems (GIS) into financial investigations allows analysts to visualize and analyze geographical data related to financial crimes. This can be particularly useful in tracking international money laundering schemes or understanding the geographic spread of fraudulent insurance claims.

Interdisciplinary Approaches

Integration of Cybersecurity: As financial systems are increasingly digital, the integration of cybersecurity into financial investigations has become essential. This involves not only protecting sensitive financial data but also understanding how cyber threats and financial crimes overlap. Financial investigators are now working closely with cybersecurity experts to address challenges like ransomware attacks, which often involve financial demands.

Collaborative Platforms: The development of collaborative platforms that facilitate information sharing across different agencies and sectors is a significant innovation. These platforms help in coordinating multi-agency investigations and leveraging expertise from various fields, leading to more efficient and effective outcomes.

Public-Private Partnerships: Strengthening partnerships between law enforcement agencies and private sector entities, such as banks and fintech companies, is crucial for timely and effective financial investigations. These partnerships enable the sharing of vital information and resources, enhancing the capabilities of all parties involved.

Regulatory and Legal Innovations

Regulatory Technology (RegTech): As financial regulations become more complex, technology solutions designed to assist companies in complying with regulations (RegTech) are becoming increasingly important. These tools can automate compliance tasks and ensure that companies adhere to international financial regulations, helping prevent legal breaches that could lead to financial crimes.

Legal Framework Enhancements: Innovations in legal frameworks, including the introduction of laws specifically targeting new types of financial crimes, are critical. For example, specific legislation addressing issues such as cryptocurrency fraud, online identity theft, and international sanctions evasion is being developed and refined.

Innovation in financial investigation is driven by the need to adapt to an ever-changing environment characterized by sophisticated financial crimes and rapid technological advancements. By embracing new technologies, methodologies, and collaborative approaches, financial investigators can enhance their ability to detect, analyze, and prevent financial crimes effectively. These innovations not only improve the technical capabilities of investigators but also foster a proactive and predictive approach to managing financial crime risks. As the field continues to evolve, ongoing education, adaptability, and interdisciplinary cooperation will be key to leveraging these innovations for future success in financial investigations.

Conclusion

As we conclude our exploration of financial investigation, it is important to reflect on the key skills and knowledge imparted throughout this book. Each chapter has been designed to equip aspiring and seasoned financial investigators with the essential tools, methodologies, and insights needed to navigate the complex landscape of financial crimes effectively. Here, we summarize these key points and encourage their application in real-world scenarios.

Foundational Skills and Knowledge:

- **The Role of Financial Investigators**: We began by understanding the crucial role financial investigators play in identifying and combating financial crimes within various sectors, including government, private industry, and non-profits. The foundational skills such as document analysis, interviewing, and surveillance form the bedrock upon which successful careers in financial investigation are built.

- **Advanced Investigative Techniques**: We delved into more sophisticated techniques like digital forensics, cryptocurrency tracing, and network analysis. These advanced tools are essential for tackling modern financial crimes that often involve complex digital components and global transactions.

- **Legal and Ethical Considerations**: A thorough grasp of legal frameworks and ethical considerations is critical for conducting investigations that are not only effective but also legally sound and ethically unimpeachable. Understanding the boundaries within which financial investigators must operate helps in navigating the often murky waters of financial crimes.

- **Crisis Management**: The skills to manage crises and high-pressure situations are invaluable, especially when dealing with high-stakes investigations that can impact significant economic or organizational interests. Learning to stay composed and make informed decisions under pressure is crucial for any investigator.

- **Emerging Trends and Future Preparedness**: Finally, we addressed the future of financial investigation, focusing on emerging trends such as the use of AI and blockchain technology, and the importance of continuous learning and adaptability in an ever-evolving field.

Application in Real-World Scenarios:

- The theoretical knowledge and practical skills covered in this book are most valuable when applied to real-world situations. Financial investigators are encouraged to leverage these tools in their daily work, whether it involves routine audits or complex transnational investigations.

- Regularly revisiting the techniques and concepts discussed, practicing them in diverse scenarios, and staying updated with the latest developments will ensure that financial investigators remain effective and relevant in their professions.

- Collaborative efforts, both within organizations and across sectors, are essential. Sharing knowledge and experiences with peers, participating in professional forums, and engaging in continuous professional development can enrich one's understanding and effectiveness as a financial investigator.

In sum, the journey through the chapters of this book provides a comprehensive toolkit that financial investigators can use to enhance their ability to uncover and address financial crimes. The encouragement to apply these skills in real-world scenarios is not just about professional growth but also about making a significant impact in safeguarding the integrity of financial systems worldwide.

The field of financial investigation is dynamic, with new challenges and technologies constantly emerging. To maintain efficacy and stay ahead in their careers, financial investigators must commit to continuing education and utilize a variety of resources available to them. This subchapter outlines the importance of ongoing learning, identifies key educational resources, and provides guidance on how to engage with these resources to enhance professional development.

Importance of Continuing Education

Staying Updated: The financial landscape is continuously evolving, with new financial products, emerging technologies, and ever-changing regulations. Continuing education helps investigators keep up with these changes, ensuring they remain effective in their roles.

Skill Enhancement: As investigative tools and techniques become more sophisticated, financial investigators need to update their skills regularly. Advanced training can provide investigators with the latest methodologies in digital forensics, data analytics, and other areas critical to modern financial investigations.

Certification Maintenance: Many professional certifications require ongoing education as a condition of renewal. These requirements are designed to ensure that professionals maintain a high standard of knowledge and competence in their field.

Key Educational Resources

Professional Associations: Organizations such as the Association of Certified Fraud Examiners (ACFE), the International Association of Financial Crimes Investigators (IAFCI), and similar groups offer a range of resources including training programs, certifications, and regular updates on industry developments. Membership in these organizations provides access to specialized knowledge and a professional community.

Workshops and Seminars: Regular attendance at workshops and seminars is a practical way to gain hands-on experience with new tools and techniques. These events often focus on specific areas of interest and provide opportunities for direct interaction with experts in the field.

Academic Courses and Webinars: Many universities and professional schools offer courses related to financial investigation and forensic accounting. Additionally, webinars allow investigators to engage with content remotely, making it easier to fit continuing education into their schedules.

Conferences: Industry conferences not only serve as a hub for learning about the latest trends and research but also provide a platform for networking with peers from around the world. These events can be invaluable for sharing experiences, strategies, and insights.

Online Learning Platforms: With the rise of digital education, many platforms now offer courses tailored to financial investigators. These platforms often include sessions on the latest software tools, legal updates, and investigative techniques.

Engaging with Educational Resources

Setting Learning Goals: To effectively engage with educational resources, investigators should set specific learning goals based on their career aspirations and the demands of their positions. This targeted approach ensures that the chosen educational activities are both relevant and beneficial.

Regular Reviews: Regularly reviewing and updating one's educational plan is crucial as career paths and industry requirements evolve. This ensures that the investigator's skills and knowledge remain at the cutting edge.

Sharing Knowledge: Upon completing educational activities, investigators should look for opportunities to share this new knowledge with their colleagues. Conducting internal training sessions or informal discussions can help disseminate new information throughout the organization, raising the overall level of expertise.

In conclusion, the path to excellence in financial investigation requires a commitment to continuous education and engagement with a broad array of resources. By staying informed, continually upgrading their skills, and actively participating in the professional community, financial investigators not only enhance their own careers but also contribute to the advancement and integrity of the field as a whole.

Final Thoughts

As we close this comprehensive exploration of financial investigation, it's important to reflect on the broader implications of this profession and the essential qualities that underpin successful practice in this field. This subchapter encapsulates the core values, the commitment to ethical standards, and the significant impact that skilled financial investigators can have on society. It also offers some parting thoughts to inspire both current and aspiring investigators to strive for excellence and integrity in their work.

The Importance of Integrity and Ethics

Upholding High Standards: Financial investigators play a critical role in maintaining the integrity of financial systems. The nature of their work often involves sensitive information and significant financial interests. Upholding the highest ethical standards is essential not only for conducting legally compliant and effective investigations but also for maintaining public trust in financial systems.

Navigating Ethical Dilemmas: Financial investigators frequently face complex ethical dilemmas. Whether it involves confidentiality issues, conflicts of interest, or the pressures of handling high-profile cases, the ability to navigate these challenges with integrity is crucial. Commitment to ongoing ethical training and a deep understanding of the legal landscape are vital for making informed, ethical decisions.

Making a Positive Impact

Contributing to Economic Stability: By detecting and preventing financial crimes, investigators contribute to the overall health and stability of the global economy. Their work helps prevent significant financial losses, supports fair business practices, and protects public and private assets.

Promoting Transparency and Accountability: Financial investigators also play a key role in promoting transparency and accountability within corporations and government entities. Their efforts ensure that these institutions operate honestly and are held accountable for their actions, which is fundamental to democratic and economic stability.

Advocating for Justice: At its core, financial investigation is about advocating for justice. Investigators help ensure that those who commit financial crimes are held accountable, which not only deters potential criminals but also fosters a culture of fairness and lawfulness.

Inspirational Closing Thoughts

Pursuit of Excellence: Aspiring and current financial investigators are encouraged to continuously strive for excellence in their field. This pursuit includes not only mastering technical skills and knowledge but also developing strong ethical judgment and a commitment to the public good.

Lifelong Learning: The field of financial investigation is ever-evolving, with new challenges and technologies constantly emerging. Embracing a philosophy of lifelong learning and adaptability is crucial for staying effective and relevant in this dynamic field.

Collaboration and Leadership: Finally, financial investigators are urged to seek opportunities for collaboration and to take on leadership roles within their professional communities. By working together and sharing knowledge, the community of financial investigators can drive innovation and effectiveness in combating financial crimes.

In conclusion, the journey through the world of financial investigation is challenging yet profoundly rewarding. It offers individuals the opportunity to make a significant impact on society, ensuring financial fairness and protecting economic systems from exploitation. As this book closes, let the principles and practices outlined here serve as a guiding light for all who seek to excel in this noble and vital profession.

List of References:

1. Financial Action Task Force (FATF) - FATF Recommendations: The International Standards on Combating Money Laundering and the Financing of Terrorism & Proliferation. [No specific publication year], FATF. Available at: http://www.fatf-gafi.org

2. Association of Certified Fraud Examiners - ACFE Fraud Examiners Manual, Association of Certified Fraud Examiners, [No specific publication year]. Available at: https://www.acfe.com

3. Sutherland, Edwin H. (1983) - White Collar Crime: The Uncut Version. Yale University Press.

4. Wells, Joseph T. (2011) - Principles of Fraud Examination, 3rd Edition. Wiley.

5. Singleton, Tommie W. (2010) - Fraud Auditing and Forensic Accounting, 4th Edition. Wiley.

6. Rezaee, Zabihollah (2002) - Financial Statement Fraud: Prevention and Detection. Wiley.

7. Golden, Thomas W., et al. (2006) - A Guide to Forensic Accounting Investigation. Wiley.

8. Albrecht, W. Steve, et al. (2012) - Fraud Examination, 4th Edition. Cengage Learning.

9. Silverstone, Howard and Sheetz, Michael (2007) - Forensic Accounting and Fraud Investigation for Non-Experts, 2nd Edition. Wiley.

10. Basel Committee on Banking Supervision - Sound Practices for the Management and Supervision of Operational Risk. [No specific publication year], Bank for International Settlements. Available at: https://www.bis.org

11. Council of Europe (1999) - Criminal Law Convention on Corruption. Council of Europe. Available at: https://www.coe.int

12. U.S. Securities and Exchange Commission - SEC Enforcement Manual. [No specific publication year], U.S. Securities and Exchange Commission. Available at: https://www.sec.gov

13. Green, Stuart P. (2006) - Lying, Cheating, and Stealing: A Moral Theory of White-Collar Crime. Oxford University Press.

14. International Monetary Fund - Spillovers in International Corporate Taxation. [No specific publication year], IMF. Available at: https://www.imf.org

15. Organisation for Economic Co-operation and Development (OECD) - Bribery and

Corruption Awareness Handbook for Tax Examiners and Tax Auditors. [No specific publication year], OECD. Available at: https://www.oecd.org

16. Gobert, James and Punch, Maurice (2003) - Rethinking Corporate Crime. Cambridge University Press.

17. United Nations Office on Drugs and Crime - Model Legislation on Money Laundering and Financing of Terrorism. [No specific publication year], UNODC. Available at: https://www.unodc.org

18. United Kingdom Serious Fraud Office - Approaches to Financial Crime Investigations. [No specific publication year], UK SFO. Available at: https://www.sfo.gov.uk

19. World Bank (2011) - The Puppet Masters: How the Corrupt Use Legal Structures to Hide Stolen Assets and What to Do About It. World Bank. Available at: https://www.worldbank.org

20. KPMG (2013) - Global Profiles of the Fraudster: Technology Enables and Weak Controls Fuel the Fraud. KPMG. Available at: https://home.kpmg

21. PwC (2020) - Global Economic Crime and Fraud Survey. PwC. Available at: https://www.pwc.com

22. Deloitte (2018) - Deloitte Forensic Center: Ten things about financial crime. Deloitte. Available at: https://www2.deloitte.com

23. Nigrini, Mark J. (2011) - Forensic Analytics: Methods and Techniques for Forensic Accounting Investigations. Wiley.

24. Calderoni, Francesco (2014) - Money Laundering Through Art: A Criminal Justice Perspective. Springer.

25. Hopwood, W. Steve, et al. (2012) - Forensic and Investigative Accounting. CCH Incorporated.

www.ingramcontent.com/pod-product-compliance
Lightning Source LLC
Chambersburg PA
CBHW052153220526
45471CB00004B/1652